Better Homes and Gardens®

decorating
ideas
under $100

Better Homes and Gardens® Books
Des Moines, Iowa

Better Homes and Gardens® Books
An imprint of Meredith® Books

Decorating Ideas Under $100
Editor: Vicki Ingham
Contributing Editor: Jilann Severson
Art Director: David Jordan
Copy Chief: Terri Fredrickson
Copy and Production Editor: Victoria Forlini
Editorial Operations Manager: Karen Schirm
Managers, Book Production: Pam Kvitne, Marjorie J. Schenkelberg
Contributing Copy Editor: Judy Friedman
Contributing Proofreaders: Kathi Di Nicola, Sue Fetters, Kenya McCullum
Indexer: Beverley Nightenhelser
Electronic Production Coordinator: Paula Forest
Editorial and Design Assistants: Kaye Chabot, Karen McFadden, Mary Lee Gavin

Meredith® Books
Publisher and Editor in Chief: James D. Blume
Design Director: Matt Strelecki
Managing Editor: Gregory H. Kayko
Executive Editor, Home Decorating and Design: Denise L. Caringer

Director, Operations: George A. Susral
Director, Production: Douglas M. Johnston
Executive Director, Sales: Ken Zagor

Vice President and General Manager: Douglas J. Guendel

Better Homes and Gardens® **Magazine**
Editor in Chief: Karol DeWulf Nickell

Meredith Publishing Group
President, Publishing Group: Stephen M. Lacy
Vice President-Publishing Director: Bob Mate

Meredith Corporation
Chairman and Chief Executive Officer: William T. Kerr

Chairman of the Executive Committee: E.T. Meredith III

All of us at Better Homes and Gardens® Books are dedicated to providing you with information and ideas to enhance your home. We welcome your comments and suggestions. Write to us at: Better Homes and Gardens Books, Home Decorating and Design Editorial Department, 1716 Locust St., Des Moines, IA 50309-3023.

If you would like to purchase any of our home decorating and design, cooking, crafts, gardening, or home improvement books, check wherever quality books are sold. Or visit us at: bhgbooks.com

It seems like we're all watching our budgets these days, keeping track of what we spend and making sure we get the most for our hard-earned dollars. At the same time, we still want a comfortable, well-decorated home with a few little luxuries. To help you achieve that goal, we've gathered some of the best decorating ideas we could find, all costing under $100 as they are shown. Who would believe custom-made items could be so affordable?

Flip through these pages to find inspiration for everything from major room overhauls to pampering little details. Whenever possible, projects start with ready-made items to make crafting easy and enjoyable. Napkins turn into pillows without any cutting or hemming. Plain curtain panels take on a designer look when dressed up with trims. Stock molding turns plain walls into attention-grabbing backgrounds. Let the manufacturers do the tedious work and save the creative part for yourself.

Expressing your own personal style has never been so much fun. Because instructions focus on the technique, personalizing each project is simple.

So whether you follow the instructions exactly or use them as a launching pad for your own design, you'll end up with a great room at a great price. Best of all, it's done by an incredible designer—you!

finishing touches

chapter 4

5

simply wonderful windows

the great outdoors

chapter 6

walls, windows, floors, and more

Paint, stock molding strips, and other staples from the home improvement center solve common decorating dilemmas on almost any surface. With a few simple strategies, long walls can appear shorter, high ceilings become a lofty focal point, backsplashes take on loads of colorful personality, and floors are suddenly more than something underfoot. New application methods and materials make it easy to transform any room.

Mold a Wall

Materials
- Tape measure
- Level or plumb line
- Hard lead pencil
- Latex paint for upper and lower wall, accent colors, and molding
- Round sponge paint applicator
- $\frac{7}{16} \times \frac{3}{8}$-inch doorstop molding
- $\frac{7}{16} \times 1\frac{1}{4}$-inch custom molding (under-cap)
- $\frac{1}{4} \times \frac{3}{4}$-inch screen molding
- Drill with small bit
- Nails
- Glue
- Wood filler

Instructions

1 Divide the wall horizontally to make it look shorter. This distance will vary with the height of the ceiling. As a general guide, follow an existing line in the room (such as a window edge) or divide the wall into fifths, making the top section one-fifth or two-fifths of the entire wall height. Draw this line around the room.

2 Paint one color above the line and a second color below the line. Apply a painted design on the lower portion. For the dots shown here, dip a round sponge paint applicator into contrasting paint. Dab it onto a paper plate to remove excess paint, then press it to the wall to create the dots.

3 The custom molding will fit along the line separating the two colors. Determine how many vertical segments you need and then cut screen molding strips to fit between the base board and where the custom molding will sit. The panels shown here are about 24 inches apart. Drill pilot holes through the screen molding, then sand and paint the screen molding.

4 Glue the screen molding to the wall and nail it in place, keeping the strips plumb.

5 Cut the custom molding to fit the wall. Drill pilot holes, then sand and paint the molding. Nail the custom molding along the top edges of the screen molding strips.

6 Cut the doorstop molding to fit across the top of the custom molding. Sand and paint the doorstop molding. Glue and nail the doorstop molding in place.

7 Fill all the nail holes, sand them if needed, and touch up the paint.

Break up a long, tall wall with two tones of paint and stock molding. Dividing the expanse into both horizontal and vertical **panels** fools the eye into thinking the wide-open space is both shorter and narrower.

Diamonds are a wall's best friend. Large diamonds scattered across a wall are one of the simplest painted finishes. Glaze mixed with the *accent* **colors and applied over the entire wall gives the room a soft, aged appearance.**

Painted Gems

Materials

- Ruler and hard lead pencil
- Lightweight cardboard
- Low-tack painter's tape
- Several colors of latex paint for the diamonds
- Off-white latex paint
- Latex glaze
- Paintbrushes
- Paint roller
- Clean lint-free rags

Instructions

1 Before starting, make sure the wall is clean and free of any residue. Draw a square onto the cardboard for the diamond template. The size of your wall and other patterns in the room will determine the diamond size. The ones shown are approximately 3 inches square. Cut out the cardboard diamond.

2 Trace diamond shapes onto the wall randomly. Use partial diamonds at corners, windows, and along the ceiling and baseboard. Mask off the diamond shapes with low-tack painter's tape. Seal the tape to the wall with a rigid plastic card.

3 For each diamond color, mix equal parts of paint, glaze, and water. Apply colors randomly. After the paint dries, carefully remove the tape.

4 Mix equal amounts of off-white paint, glaze, and water. Roll this mixture over the wall, working in small sections. Using a rag, blot off most of the top coat for a softened effect. While the first section is still wet, move to the next section. Overlap the lines and blot them well so the wall has an even look and there are no visible joints.

Stripe It Rich

Materials

- Ruler, level, and straightedge
- Light and dark latex paint in related hues
- Low-tack painter's tape
- Textured paint in a darker contrasting color
- Paint roller and pan, plain roller covers, ⅜-inch nap roller cover

Instructions

1 Paint the entire wall the lightest color. After the paint dries, use the ruler, level, and straightedge to mark off stripes of differing widths. The stripes shown measure 6, 12, 18, and 30 inches but smaller walls will need to be done in proportionally narrower stripes.

2 Mask off the widest stripes and paint them the darker color. When the paint dries, remove the tape.

3 Mask off the two mid-size widths of stripes. Using the ⅜-inch nap roller and following the manufacturer's instructions, paint these stripes with the textured paint. For the best results, use one even coat from top to bottom and avoid overlapping lines.

4 When the paint dries, remove the tape. The light base-coat color will form the narrow stripes along the wall.

colors

A trio of deep **colors** gives an elegant look to a formerly plain wall. Textured paint for the darkest stripes adds to the mix, catching the light differently than the other two colors. Look for textured paints at paint and home improvement stores.

Flower power lives on. Dauber sponges **used for painting and stenciling are easily cut into simple shapes and used to create a budding design. A small dauber forms the flower center while a large one makes the petals.**

Field of Flowers

Materials
- Large and small sponge-style paint daubers (available at crafts, paint, and home improvement stores)
- Fine-tipped permanent marker
- Small scissors
- 2 colors of acrylic or latex paint
- Paper plates

Instructions

1 Draw six petal shapes onto the large dauber (see the photograph *at left*). Cut along the lines, then pull away the sections between the petals.

2 Lightly dip the petal-shaped dauber into paint and dab it onto a paper plate to remove excess paint. Press the dauber onto the wall. Repeat, reloading the dauber as needed and spacing the petals randomly along the wall.

3 After the paint dries, dip the small dauber into the contrasting paint. Blot it onto a paper plate to remove the excess paint and use that shape to form the flower centers.

Go Dotty

Materials

- 2 large sponge-style paint daubers (available at crafts, paint, and home improvement stores)
- Fine-tipped permanent marker
- Small scissors
- 2 contrasting colors of acrylic or latex paint
- Paper plates

Instructions

1 Using a marker, draw a row of scallops around the outer edge of one dauber. Draw another row of scallops around the center, forming a ring. Snip along the lines, forming wavy edges (see the photograph *at right*).

2 Lightly dip the plain dauber into the darker paint. Tap it onto a paper plate to remove most of the paint. Lightly press the dauber to the wall to create a dot design. Reload the dauber with paint and repeat stamping, spacing the dots randomly across the wall.

3 After the dots dry, stamp the rings over the dots in the same manner. Offset some of the rings slightly so that a rim of darker color shows along part of the outer edge.

Stamp out boredom with not-your-average polka dots. One dauber sponge makes a basic dot design. A second dauber with the center and edge snipped away forms a ring that gives an artistic look to the spots, especially when slightly offset.

Photocopies of botanical prints fill a wall with images *opposite*, giving it the look of an English garden room. Books and calendars often carry page after page of noncopyrighted images. Adapt the size of the prints on a photocopier or computer scanner so that they all match, then print them on good-quality paper and decoupage them to the wall.

border

Create the look of an imported tile border without much expense or expertise. Photocopy or scan a real tile or noncopyrighted images that resemble tile and apply them directly to the wall, edging them with a row of braid.

Paper Tiles

Materials

- Ruler, level, and straightedge
- Color copies of noncopyrighted images
- Clear spray sealer
- Decoupage medium
- Decorative braid
- Liquid ravel preventer
- Hot-glue gun

Instructions

1 Photocopy or scan and print the images, adjusting the sizes so they all match. Trim away the excess margins and spray the images with spray sealer for protection.

2 Using a level and straightedge, mark the bottom line for the images on the wall. For chair-rail height, mark 32 to 36 inches up from the floor. The tile also can be lined up with mirrors, windows, or other elements in the room. Tape the prints to the wall. If

desired, place images around mirrors, windows, or doors.

3 Working with one image at a time, remove the print from the wall, apply decoupage medium to the back, and smooth the print in place. Repeat for remaining prints.

4 Cut braid to fit along the top and bottom edges of the "tiles." Treat the edges of the braid with liquid ravel preventer. Hot-glue the braid in place.

Prints Charming

Materials

- Ruler and level
- Color copies of noncopyrighted prints
- Color copy of a frame or clip art borders cut and mitered to form a frame
- Clear spray sealer
- Decoupage medium

Instructions

1 Determine the size and placement of the prints and mark their positions on the wall. Photocopy or scan and print the images, adjusting sizes as needed. Trim away margins and spray the images with spray sealer to protect them from moisture and soil.

2 Photocopy one frame to fit all the images. If a print of a frame is not available, photocopy a clip art border. Cut and miter the border to form a frame.

3 Tape the copies to the wall, making adjustments as necessary. Remove one image at a time. Coat the back with decoupage medium and smooth it onto the wall. Repeat for all the images.

4 After the prints dry, glue the frames over the images in the same manner.

images

Make a grand statement in a small space by decoupaging full-size

posters over a painted or wallpapered wall. Look for coordinating posters at framing or art supply stores, or check online sources. The sizes can vary as long as the theme, scale, and colors remain related. Border the posters with frames of grosgrain ribbon.

Poster Power

Materials
- Large posters
- Clear spray sealer suitable for paper
- Wallpaper paste or decoupage medium
- Wallpaper sponge or soft rag
- Level and ruler
- ½-inch-wide grosgrain ribbon
- Thick white crafts glue
- 4 upholstery tacks per poster

Instructions
1 Trim away margins from the posters, then spray the fronts with two coats of spray sealer to protect them against soil and moisture.

2 Using a level and ruler, mark the placement of each poster. Align the centers of the posters, keeping those of matching sizes at the same height.

3 Coat the back of the posters with wallpaper paste or decoupage medium. Use vinyl-to-vinyl wallpaper paste if you are adhering the posters to a wallpapered wall. Lay the posters in place, then press them to the wall and smooth out any air bubbles with a wallpaper sponge or a soft rag. Immediately wipe away any excess adhesive according to the manufacturer's directions.

4 Cut ribbon to fit each edge of each poster, then glue it around the edge for a frame. Place a decorative tack at each corner.

Spicy Decoupage
Materials
- Photocopies or scans of noncopyrighted prints, scaled to the proper size
- Clear spray sealer appropriate for paper
- Ruler and straightedge
- Wallpaper paste or decoupage medium
- Wallpaper sponge or soft rag
- Print papers for backgrounds (optional)
- Small decorative chain
- Decorative picture hook
- 2 decorative upholstery tacks
- Ribbon for bow or bow design cut from decorative paper

Instructions
1 Trim away the margins, leaving a small white border to serve as a frame on some of the copies. Cut background papers to make frames for the center image and any other desired prints. Spray all the papers with two or more coats of clear sealer to protect them against soil and moisture.

2 Mark the placement of each image on the wall using a level and straightedge. Apply wallpaper paste or decoupage medium to the back of each image, then press it to the wall. Smooth the print in place with a wallpaper sponge or a soft rag. Remove any excess glue immediately. For images with a background print, glue the decorative paper to the wall first and let it dry. Center the

image over the paper and glue it in place.
Note: Use vinyl-to-vinyl wallpaper paste if you
are applying the images over wallpaper.

3 If you are using a paper bow, glue it above
the main image as shown *above*. Place a
decorative hook over the bow. For a ribbon
bow, use a tack to hold it in place. Loop a
chain over the hook as shown *above right*.
Tack the ends of the chain to the upper
corners of the main image.

**Create a kitchen collage from seed packets, advertising,
cookbook or garden illustrations, or small posters and
prints. Here herbs provide a general theme, but choose any
motif that matches your decorating style. A color
photocopier or computer scanner and printer make it easy to
bring all the images to proper scale. A picture chain adds a
bit of whimsy to the arrangement.**

whimsy

Botanical Backsplash

Materials

- Botanical images from calendars, books, prints, or posters
- Spackling compound and sandpaper
- Decoupage medium
- Wallpaper sponge or soft rag
- Clear satin-finish polyurethane

Instructions

1 Prepare the wall by filling any cracks or holes. Sand the wall and wipe it clean.

2 Make copies of the prints using a color photocopier or scanner and printer. Adjust the sizes as needed so the images will fit together tightly. Trim away excess background, keeping the edges perfectly straight so they will butt together.

3 Coat the backs of the papers with decoupage medium. Smooth the papers to the wall with a wallpaper sponge or a soft rag, removing any air bubbles. Wipe away excess adhesive immediately.

4 When dry, apply two or more coats of clear polyurethane for protection. Reapply the polyurethane as needed over time.

Painterly prints clipped or copied from calendars or books give a kitchen backsplash an Old World look. The designs fit the wall in a *collage* fashion so the pattern is dense, with few blank spaces. Polyurethane seals and protects the wall from water damage.

The Last Lath

Materials

- Textural wood strips such as lath, beadboard, barn wood, or siding
- Saw with miter capabilities
- Sandpaper
- Clear satin-finish polyurethane

Instructions

1 To determine the angle of the boards, tape paper to the backsplash area and draw the desired slant of the lines. Mark the top and bottom to determine the cutting angle. The laths shown are cut at 60 degrees, but almost any angle can be used.

2 Cut out the boards according to your pattern. Adjust for differences in cabinet heights and at corners.

3 Nail the strips in place using finish nails. Lightly sand the wood, then wipe it clean with a tack cloth. Apply two or more coats of polyurethane.

Common plaster laths come to the forefront of a kitchen wall when used as a backsplash. Sanding along with a couple coats of polyurethane smooth out the rough surface and make cleaning easier.

Tile Cross-Stitch

Materials

- Graph paper
- Grease pencil
- Tile adhesive, grout, and tile sealer
- Mesh-backed ¾-inch ceramic or glass tiles in white, red, pink, medium green and light green
- Trowel, sponges, and other tile-setting tools

Instructions

1 Draw out the dimensions of your backsplash onto the graph paper. Chart the rose pattern *at left* onto the graph paper, adjusting the spacing as needed.

2 Following the pattern, use a grease pencil to mark the white tiles, indicating the placement of each of the colored tiles. Carefully remove all the marked tiles from the mesh background.

3 Apply the tile adhesive to the prepared wall according to the manufacturer's

Small mesh-backed tiles make creating an intricate *floral* pattern quick and easy. Simply pop out a few of the white background tiles and replace them with different colors to make the garden-fresh pattern.

directions. Press the mesh-backed tiles onto the wall. While the adhesive is still wet press the colored tiles into the open spaces following your pattern. Make sure the replacement tiles are straight and even.

4 After the adhesive dries, apply grout according to the manufacturer's directions. Seal the tile to protect the grout from stains.

Shard Art

Materials

- Whole or broken tiles, plates, small flowerpots, pottery pieces and shards, snippets of screen, rocks, marbles, and other desired items
- Old terry cloth towels
- Tile nippers (available for rent at many tile stores)
- Mastic or similar heavy-duty adhesive appropriate for walls and tiles
- Floor grout
- Sand
- Trowel, sponges, and other tile-setting tools
- Polyurethane

Instructions

1. Set aside some tiles to be left whole, especially if they have an interesting color or pattern. To break the remaining large items into smaller pieces, wrap each item in a towel and strike it with a hammer until it breaks into the desired sizes.

2. Lay the items out on the floor to establish the pattern. Rebreak any items as needed. Use tile nippers to create small pieces and remove any jagged edges.

3. Apply the adhesive to the wall following the manufacturer's directions. Press the mosaic in place. Support heavy objects with small nails until the adhesive dries and the item is held tightly in place. Remove the nails when the adhesive dries.

4. Mix the floor grout, thinning it slightly with water. Add sand for texture. Apply the grout according to the manufacturer's directions. If necessary, wear plastic gloves and use your fingers to work the grout into small spaces.

5. After the grout dries, seal the mosaic with two coats of polyurethane.

A smorgasbord of tiles, shards, flowerpots, and found objects becomes a work of art when arranged on a wall in a random pattern. Use tiles from previous projects or check home improvement stores for odds and ends, adding garage sale pottery, damaged dinnerware, or whatever else strikes your fancy.

It's All Diamonds

Materials

- Tape measure and straightedge
- Low-tack painter's tape
- Paints: base color, metallic glaze, and border color or as desired
- Wallpaper brush or faux finish tools

Instructions

1 Draw one large square in the center of the ceiling, placing it on the diagonal to form a diamond. Add a square of equal size on each side so the points touch. Mask off the outer 1½ inches with painter's tape. Seal the tape to the ceiling with a rigid plastic card.

2 Apply the base coat. After the paint dries, add a coat of metallic glaze. While the glaze is still wet, run a wallpaper brush or other faux finish tool through the glaze to create a textured finish.

3 After the glaze dries, mask off the outer 1½-inch border and paint the border strip, using a contrasting color.

Painted diamonds add interest to the ceiling and also make a narrow room appear slightly wider. The faux-finish diamonds shown *above* **are created with a wallpaper brush, but plain paint also will yield an attractive result.**

Texture Overhead

Materials

- Measuring tape and straightedge
- Embossed wallpaper and matching embossed border paper
- Wallpaper paste and tools (this may vary with the paper brand; follow the wallpaper manufacturer's directions)
- Narrow decorative molding strips
- Finish nails
- Paint in the desired colors

Instructions

1 Draw a large square or diamond in the center of the ceiling. Measure the width of the border and draw it inside the diamond. Cut the wallpaper to fit this inner dimension.

2 Hang the wallpaper according to the manufacturer's directions. Instructions and materials often vary between paper brands, so follow the instructions carefully. You may need to piece a large diamond.

3 Hang the border around the diamond, mitering the corners. If desired, paint or glaze the wallpaper and border.

4 Cut the molding strips to fit around the outer edge of the border, mitering the corners. Paint the molding, then nail it over the edge of the border. Fill the nail holes and retouch the paint.

Mimic the look of an expensive plasterwork ceiling accent with embossed wallpaper and a coordinating border. The pricey textured paper that used to be available only through decorators is now on shelves at home improvement centers at a reasonable cost.

Ceiling Frame

Materials

- 3 sizes of molding strips, including crown molding
- Saw with miter capabilities
- Paint in white and three closely related shades
- Low-tack painter's tape

Instructions

1. Cut the moldings to fit the room, mitering the corners. Place the crown molding at the outer edge and use narrower moldings as you work inward. Keep the crown and middle molding square with the room. If desired, shape the narrow innermost molding with inverted-notched corners. Paint the molding.

2. Mark the molding placement on the ceiling. Mask off the sections of the ceiling with painter's tape and paint each section.

3. Nail the molding to the ceiling along the lines. Fill the nail holes and retouch the paint.

Victorian homes often highlighted a chandelier with a shaped ceiling. Create the same effect with molding strips and paint. The rows of molding strips become progressively narrower and the paint color changes with each band.

embossed

A Tin Line

Materials

- Tape measure and straightedge
- Embossed wallpaper
- Wallpaper paste and tools (this may vary with the paper brand; follow the wallpaper manufacturer's directions)
- Paint (metallic colors will best mimic the look of a tin ceiling)
- Paintbrushes and roller
- Molding strips, such as crown or chair rail molding
- Saw with miter capabilities

Instructions

1 Draw a line along the wall 12 inches down from the ceiling. Prepare this section of the wall and the entire ceiling for wallpapering. Wallpaper brands differ in materials and application techniques. Read and follow the manufacturer's instructions carefully.

2 Hang the wallpaper on the wall and ceiling. Paint the wallpaper the desired color. Metallic or pearlized paint will give the impression of a tin ceiling, but any paint will work. See the wallpaper instructions for suggestions and painting directions.

3 Cut the molding to fit the room, mitering the corners. Paint the molding, then nail it in place. Fill the nail holes and retouch the paint.

Because they've become so trendy, old ceiling tins have become expensive and rare. Create the same look with embossed wallpaper. Cover the entire ceiling, then extend a band down the wall and cap it with crown molding.

stencil

Create the same impact as a floor rug without worrying about the mat slip-sliding away. Painting an imperfect wood floor covers small flaws. A stenciled garland of leaves and branches sets off a section of a room in much the same way an area rug would.

Border Appeal

Materials

- Paintable wood filler
- Hand-held sponge sander and sandpaper
- Liquid floor cleaner and wax remover
- Latex floor paint for base coat
- Paint pads, brushes, or rollers
- Clean lint-free paint rags or stencil brushes
- Hard lead pencil
- Acrylic or latex paint for stencil design
- Stencil plastic and crafts knife
- Spray stencil adhesive
- Satin-finish polyurethane floor sealer
- Pad-style paint applicators

Instructions

1 Remove any old wax and floor varnish. Remove staples and pound in raised nails. Fill any nail holes and small gouges or scratches with wood filler. Sand the entire floor lightly and clean it with floor cleaner.

2 Paint the floor with a base coat of floor paint. For an opaque look, apply two or more coats of paint. For a lighter "pickled" look, paint the floor and then wipe away some of the paint before it dries.

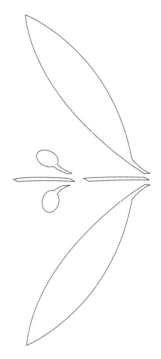

3 Using a pencil, lightly draw the guideline for your stenciled design. Enlarge the design *at right* on a photocopier to the desired size. Trace the design onto stencil plastic and cut it out with a crafts knife. *Tip:* To protect your work surface and make cutting easier, cut on a self-healing rotary cutter mat or a piece of glass. Spray the back of the stencil with stencil adhesive according to the manufacturer's directions.

4 Align the stencil with the guideline on the floor. For a soft design like the one shown, dampen a rag and wring it dry. Dip it into the contrasting paint and blot it on paper towels until very little paint remains. Dab the paint through the stencil openings as shown *at right*. Repeat until the entire guideline is covered, adapting the design to fit as you work. For a bolder, more solid design, lightly dip a stencil brush into the paint. Tap it onto a paper plate until very little paint remains. Pounce the brush over the stencil opening to transfer the paint to the floor.

5 After the paint dries completely, seal it with two or more coats of satin polyurethane floor sealer. A pad-style applicator will provide the most even coverage.

The design on a vinyl floor often looks dated long before the floor shows wear.

Update the pattern with paint and a stamped design. Check paint departments for a primer designed specifically for vinyl, latex floor paint, and floor-quality polyurethane. They're the keys to making the new design withstand wear and tear.

Vinyl Facelift

Materials

- Liquid sanding solution
- Primer for vinyl surfaces
- Paint brush and roller
- Latex floor paint in two colors
- Deep-cut rubber stamp (often called decorator stamps)
- Wedge-shaped cosmetic sponge
- Floor-quality water-based polyurethane

Instructions

1 Clean the floor and remove any wax. Apply liquid sanding solution according to the manufacturer's directions. This will roughen the surface and help the paint adhere. Paint the floor with vinyl primer and let it dry.

2 Apply two coats of latex floor paint in the base color, letting the paint dry completely between coats.

3 Pour a small amount of the accent color floor paint onto a paper plate. Using the wedge-shaped sponge, dab the paint onto the stamp. Take care not to apply too much paint or let it seep into the depressed areas of the design. Stamp the image onto the floor in a random pattern, reloading the stamp surface as needed.

4 When the paint is dry, cover the floor with two coats of polyurethane to protect the paint. Let each coat dry completely.

Letter-Perfect

Materials

- Paintable wood filler
- Hand-held sponge sander and sandpaper
- Liquid floor cleaner and wax remover
- Latex floor paint in two colors
- Paint pads, brushes, or rollers
- Large pre-cut stencils
- Spray stencil adhesive
- Stencil brushes
- Satin-finish polyurethane floor sealer
- Pad-style paint applicators

Instructions

1 Prepare and base coat the floor as described in steps 1 and 2 of the painted floor shown on *pages 24 and 25*.

Perk up a worn wood floor with **paint** **and a scattering of stenciled letters and numbers. If the ABCs and 123s don't suit your style, look for other pre-cut stencils or cut your own using simple die-cut shapes (available at crafts and scrapbooking stores) as the pattern.**

2 Randomly scatter the stencils over the floor, adjusting the spacing and placement as desired. Secure the stencils to the floor using stencil adhesive.

3 Pour a small amount of the accent paint onto a paper plate. Dip the tip of the stencil brush into the paint, then dab it onto another plate to remove most of the paint. Tap the paint through the stencil and onto the floor.

4 When the design is complete and the paint is dry, seal the floor with two or more coats of polyurethane. A pad-style applicator will provide the most even coverage.

Replacing a plain patio or floor with paver bricks is both costly and tricky. Mimic the look on a concrete floor with concrete stain and kitchen sponges. Before starting, check out existing brick surfaces for inspiration. New brick patterns are usually precise while older brickwork is often uneven in both spacing and size. Incorporate your favorite ideas into your design.

concrete

Painted Bricks

Materials

- Commercial concrete cleaner and etcher
- Tape measure and straightedge
- Low-tack painter's tape, rigid plastic card
- Kitchen sponges
- Silicon acrylic concrete stain in brick red and light buff
- Paint brushes and rollers

Instructions

1. Clean and etch the concrete with commercial concrete cleaner and etcher. Instructions vary with the brand, so follow the manufacturer's directions and safety precautions exactly. Let dry 72 hours.

2. Measure the outer border and mask off the center. Draw out your brick pattern. Use painter's tape to create the mortar spaces between the bricks. Seal the tape to the concrete with a piece of rigid plastic.

3. Cut sponges to fit the various brick sizes. Dampen the sponges, then wring them dry. Dip a sponge in brick red stain. Blot it on paper towels to remove excess stain. Press the sponge to the floor to create a brick. Repeat until all the brick spaces are stained. Let the stain dry 24 hours.

4. Repeat the process with the light buff stain to add highlights to each brick. Using very little stain and pressure, stamp directly over the first bricks. Let the stain dry 24 hours. Remove the tape. The exposed concrete will resemble mortar.

5. Mask off the outer border. Paint it with red brick stain. Let the stain dry 24 hours.

Have a Hearth

Materials
- Several large floor tiles in a prominent color
- Small floor tiles in neutral colors
- Old terry cloth towels
- Hammer
- Tile nippers (often available for rent from tile stores)
- Tile adhesive, floor grout, and tile sealer
- Trowel, sponges, and other tile-setting tools

Instructions
1. Prepare the hearth surface according to the directions on the tile adhesive package. Draw out the hearth shape on kraft paper.

2. Wrap a single large tile in terry cloth towels and break it with a hammer into several pieces. Carefully uncover the pieces and reassemble the tile on the paper pattern, leaving small spaces between the broken pieces. Repeat for the remaining large tiles. Leave a large space between each tile.

3. Break the small tiles in the same manner. Fill in the open spaces with the small pieces. Trim the pieces and remove jagged edges with tile nippers.

4. Apply tile adhesive to the hearth. Transfer the tile pieces to the adhesive, starting at one end and working across, following the pattern you have designed. After the adhesive dries, grout the tiles following the manufacturer's directions. Seal the finished hearth to keep the grout from staining.

Large floor tiles that are broken apart, then pieced back together form the focal point for a *mosaic* hearth. The spaces between are filled with smaller shards, all done in a neutral color scheme.

furniture fix-ups

Your furnishings*, much like your wardrobe, may start to look dated long before they are ready to be tossed. Give small pieces a new sense of style with slipcovers, trims, or finishing* touches*. Flea markets, garage sales, unfinished furniture sources, and even crafts and home improvement stores often offer up pieces that have good lines, but are in dire need of a* makeover.

Simple Skirt

Materials
- Approximately ⅔ yard lightweight fabric per chair (this will vary with the chair size)
- Water-erasable fabric marker
- Fusible adhesive tape or sewing thread
- Ribbon, string, or twine for corner ties

Instructions

1 Center the fabric over the chair seat, letting it fall over the front and side (apron) pieces and just beyond the top of the chair legs. Draw the desired hemline and mark any points that need to be notched to fit the chair legs and back.

2 Remove the fabric. Straighten the lines and mark a cutting line 1 inch beyond the hemline. Cut out the skirt.

3 Press up the edges, clipping corners as needed. Fuse or topstitch the hem.

4 Place the skirt back on the chair. Tack the ties to the corners. Use the front ties to gather up the excess fabric at the corners, arranging the folds softly. Use the back ties to anchor the cover to the back of the chair.

skirt

A flirty little skirt adds softness to a curvy dining chair. It's a perfect way to hide a seat that no longer matches your *decor* or is showing some wear. Best of all, this low-sew project is so easy you can make different skirts for every season or occasion.

dressy

If the lines of a chair are too pretty to hide but you want to soften the look, tie on a filmy cover. It will let the fine architecture show through while adding a dressy touch.

Sheer Cover-Up

Materials
- Tape measure
- Kraft paper for a pattern
- Sheer fabric with good body (the amount will vary with the chair size)
- Water-erasable fabric marker
- Grommets and grommet tool
- 2-inch-wide sheer ribbon for ties

Instructions

1 Measure the chair and make the pattern as described for the Pretty Pinafore on *page 33*, ignoring references to the scallops and curved top.

2 Assemble the chair cover as described for the Pretty Pinafore on *page 33*. When working with sheer fabric, always turn the raw edges of the seam allowances and hems under twice to encase the raw edges.

3 Place the cover over the chair. Mark the placement for the grommets using the photograph as a guide. Install the grommets according to the package directions. Lace ribbon through the grommets to secure the cover to the chair.

The scalloped edge at the bottom of this cover is a perfect match for the **curves** on both the top and the legs of the chair. For chairs that already have lots of shape and detail, small prints are the best choice for a cover fabric.

Pretty Pinafore

Materials

- Tape measure
- Kraft paper for a pattern
- Medium-weight fabric (the amount will vary with the chair size)
- Water-erasable fabric marker
- Ribbon, twine, or string for ties

Instructions

1 This cover is made from a long panel that goes over the chair back and seat in one continuous strip. Shorter side panels are added at the seat edges. For the main panel, start measuring at the back of the chair. Beginning at the seat top, measure up the back, across the chair top, down the front of the chair back, and across the seat to the front edge of the chair. Add 5 inches to each end. For the width of this panel, use the seat width. Make a paper pattern following these measurements.

2 For each side panel, measure the seat from front to back. Each side panel will be 5 inches long. Cut a paper pattern following these measurements.

3 To make the scalloped edges, divide the lower edges of the pattern panels into three even scallops. Place the pattern over the chair. *Note:* The curved top edge will be shaped later. Make adjustments as needed.

4 Lay the pattern on the fabric. Using a fabric marker, add the following measurements to the pattern pieces: 1 inch for seam allowances on all straight edges of the main panel; 5 additional inches to each end of the main panel; 1-inch seam allowances to the short and upper edges of the side panels; 5 additional inches to the lower edges of the side panels. Cut out all pieces. Do not cut scallops.

5 With right sides facing, turn up 5 inches on each short edge of the main panel and the lower edge of each side panel. Transfer the scallop shape to the folded edge. Sew along the marked line. Trim the seam allowances and clip the curves. Turn the side panels to the right sides and press. Set them aside. Working on the main panel, with the wrong side face out, slip the main panel over the chair. Using a fabric marker, trace the upper curved edge. Remove the cover and baste along this line. Put the cover back on the chair and check the fit of the upper edge. When you are satisfied with the fit, sew along the basting line. Trim the seam allowances and clip the curves. Turn the cover to the right side and press.

6 Place the cover on the chair. Lay a side panel on the seat, aligning the raw edge with the raw edge of the main panel. Pin the panels together along the seamline. Repeat for the remaining panel. Remove the cover and sew the panels in place.

7 Hem the remaining raw edges. Arrange the slipcover on the chair. Tack ties to the lower corners and back edges as shown.

Fancy Folding Chairs

Materials

- Measuring tape
- Water-erasable fabric marker
- 54-inch-wide medium-weight fabric (the amount will vary with the chair size)
- 12-inch lengths of ⅝-inch-wide grosgrain ribbon, totaling 5½ yards (may be several coordinating colors)

Instructions

Note: Two long, flat panels (a main panel running front to back and a side panel running across the chair seat and to the floor) cover this folding chair. The panels overlap where they cross the seat, adding extra padding. Make the panels longer than the chair measurements so they sweep the floor as shown, or cut them to barely touch the floor.

1 To determine the size of the main panel, start at the back of the chair. Measure from the floor, up the back of the chair, across the top, down the front of the chair back, across the seat, and back to the floor. Add 4 inches for hemming and 4 more inches if a sweep is desired. For the width, measure the width of the chair seat and add 8 inches for hems. Cut out this panel.

2 For the side panel, measure from the floor up to the seat, across the seat, and back to the floor. Add 4 inches for hems and another 4 inches if a sweep is desired. For the width of this panel, measure the depth of the seat and add 8 inches. Cut out this panel.

3 Turn under ¼ inch, then 3¾ inches on each long side of the main panel and pin to secure. On the short edges, turn under 1 inch twice and pin. Repeat for the side panel.

4 Center the side panel across the chair seat. Lay the main panel over the chair, pinning it to hold it in place if necessary. Make any needed adjustments to ensure that the cover is perfectly centered. Pin the side and main panels together along the seat edges. Mark the edges of the seat with the water-erasable fabric marker.

5 Remove the cover and topstitch the two panels together along the marked seat edges. Topstitch all edges and hems.

6 Slip the cover over the chair. Tack the ribbons to the chair in pairs as shown and tie the cover in place.

Who would suspect that an ordinary **folding** chair hides underneath this sweeping cover? Sew two flat panels together and tie them in place with ribbon. The covers fold up as flatly and neatly as the chair itself.

A tall, slim chair takes on a whole new **look** with a change of dress. Awning stripes lend a casual air and echo the straight lines. Toile suggests a more formal feeling, while a bold, bright floral blooms with fun and funky appeal. There's a secret here: The side panels are removable if you prefer to show a little leg.

Straight Shift

Materials

- Measuring tape
- Water-erasable fabric marker
- 54-inch-wide medium-weight fabric (the amount will vary with the chair size)
- Self-adhesive hook-and-loop tape

Instructions

Note: Two long, flat panels (a main panel running front to back and a side panel running across the chair seat and to the floor on each side) cover this chair. The panels overlap where they cross the seat. Hook-and-loop tape fastens the two sections together so the side panels can be removed.

1 To determine the size of the main panel, start at the back of the chair. Measure from the floor, up the back of the chair, across the top, down the front of the chair back, across the seat, and back to the floor. Add a 1½-inch hem to each end. For the width of this panel, measure between the rails of the chair and add a 1-inch hem to each side. Cut out this panel. Hem all sides, encasing the raw edges.

2 For the side panel, measure from the floor up to the seat, across the seat, and back to the floor. Add a 1½-inch hem to each end. For the width of this panel, measure the space between the legs and add a 1-inch hem to each end. Cut out this panel. Hem all sides, encasing the raw edges.

3 Cut four 17×2½-inch strips for ties. With right sides facing, fold each tie in half lengthwise and stitch along the raw edges, leaving an opening for turning. Turn the tie right side out and slipstitch the opening closed. Press the ties.

4 Lay the main panel over the chair. Mark the tie placement where the seat and back meet. Tack the ties in place and tie the panel to the chair.

5 Center the seat panel under the main panel. Cut hook-and-loop tape to fit along the seat edges. Apply the soft-loop side of the tape to the underside of the top panel. Apply the rigid-hook side of the tape to the right side of the side panel. Join the two panels.

Bistro Style

Materials

- Tape measure
- Polyester quilt batting
- Fabric for the cover (the amount will vary with the size of the chair)
- Fabric glue
- Self-adhesive hook-and-loop tape
- 3½ yards cording or ribbon for ties

Instructions

Note: Two flat panels (one running front-to-back, one running side-to-side) cover the chair seat. The panels overlap where they cross the seat. Hook-and-loop tape holds the two sections together so the side panels can be removed.

1 Cut batting to wrap over the chair back. Cut fabric twice the length and twice the width of the batting. Center the batting on the wrong side of the fabric and tack it in place with dots of fabric glue. Fold the top and bottom edges of the fabric over the batting so they meet at the center. slipstitch or glue them in place. Fold the side edges of the fabric to the center in the same manner and slipstitch or glue them in place. The top pad is now completely encased in fabric.

2 Fold the back cover in half and lay it over the chair back. Tack 16-inch-long ties to each lower corner and tie the cover in place.

3 Measure the chair seat from front to back and add a 6- to 8-inch drop on each end. Cut batting to this measurement. Measure the chair seat from side to side and add the same amount of drop to each end. Cut batting to this measurement.

4 Cut fabric twice the width and twice the length of each batting piece. Cover each piece of seat batting with fabric in the same manner as the back cover.

5 Center the side-to-side piece on the seat. Center the front-to-back piece over it. Cut hook-and-loop tape to fit along the edges of the chair seat. Adhere the soft-loop side of the tape to the underside of the top panel. Adhere the rigid-hook side to the right side of the other panel. Press the panels together.

Bistro chairs are unbeatable for style and convenience, but they often lack comfort. Soften the look and feel of a traditional bistro chair with lightly padded covers.

This seat cover fits to a T—or whatever letter you choose. Use computer fonts for the letter patterns, then **appliqué** them to a tailored seat cover. Use one matching monogram for all the chairs, or give each seat an initial of its own.

Monogrammed Skirt

Materials

- Tape measure
- Kraft paper for pattern
- 54-inch-wide medium-weight fabric (about 3 yards, but the amount will vary with the chair)
- Computer-generated letter for monogram (the one shown measures 10×7 inches)
- Contrasting nonwoven (nonfraying) fabric for monogram, such as imitation suede
- Paper-backed fusible adhesive material
- 2 yards ¼-inch diameter piping

Instructions

1 Measure the chair according to the diagram *below*. For the skirt width, double the seat depth and add the seat front width, plus 36 inches for the box pleats, back closure, and hems. For the skirt length, measure the seat height and add 2½ inches for seam allowances and hem.

2 Trace the seat shape onto paper. Extend the seat shape 20 inches in the back to create a flap that will hang to the floor with a 2-inch hem. Make small notches in this piece to fit around the chair structure (see the Fabric Cutting Diagram *below right* for the pattern shape). Cut out the pattern and fit it over the chair. Adjust as needed. Add ½-inch seam allowances to all sides.

3 Cut out the seat and skirt pieces. Cut four 12×1-inch ties. Use the remaining fabric for bias strips for matching piping, if desired.

4 Fuse the paper-backed adhesive material to the wrong side of the monogram fabric. Trace the letter onto the fabric and cut it out. Peel off the backing, center the letter over the seat, and fuse it in place according to the manufacturer's directions. If desired, machine satin stitch around the letter with a wide, tight zigzag stitch.

5 Baste self-made or purchased piping to the front and sides of the seat piece along the seamline.

6 Hem the long bottom edge and short side edges of the skirt. With right sides facing and raw edges aligned, pin the center of the skirt to the center front of the seat. Continue pinning toward the corners. At the front corners, fold back 3 inches of skirt fabric and pin the fold in place. Fold the fabric forward again to make half a box pleat. Pin the fold in place at the corner. Repeat on the other side of the corner, reversing the directions of the folds (see the diagram *at right*). The outer folds should meet perfectly at the seat corner. Continue pinning the skirt around the seat.

7 To make the ties, hem the short edges. Turn the long edges under ¼ inch, then fold the ties in half lengthwise to encase the raw edges. Topstitch along both long edges. Slip the cover over the chair. Tack one end of one tie to the top of the skirt back and a second tie to the center of the skirt back. Tack the remaining ties in place. Flip the back flap of the seat through the opening in the chair and over the skirt back of the skirt (see the photograph *opposite*).

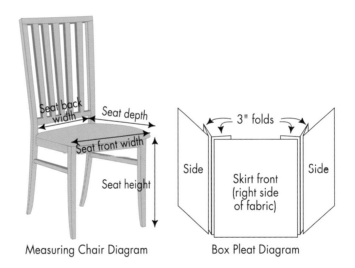

Measuring Chair Diagram

Box Pleat Diagram

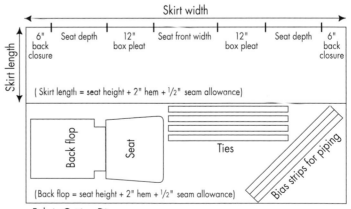

Fabric Cutting Diagram

Add a mantel-like surface as well as architectural interest with a corbel-based shelf. Look for vintage brackets at **antiques** shops, flea markets, and salvage houses. Reproduction corbels are available at home improvement centers. Just add a narrow board for the top.

Simple Sideboard

Materials

- Vintage or reproduction corbels
- Pine board for the shelf (the size will vary with the corbel and room size)
- Latex and acrylic paints to match the corbels or as desired
- Faux finishing tools, if desired
- Screws
- Finish nails
- Paintable wood filler
- Satin-finish polyurethane (optional)

Instructions

1 Determine the placement of the corbels, aligning them with studs if possible. Cut the

shelf to the proper size for this spacing. Paint the shelf. To blend the shelf with vintage corbels, study the colors and layers of paint on the corbels and duplicate them as closely as possible on the shelf. Use a rag to wipe off excess paint, a dry brush to leave a streaked effect, and sanding to make the piece look worn. Check paint supply departments for faux-finish and aged-finish tools and paints.

2 To age new corbels and a shelf, check paint supply departments for paints, glazes, and kits that produce aged finishes. Each manufacturer is different, so always use compatible products and follow the manufacturer's directions exactly.

3 Position the corbels on the wall ¾ inch lower than the shelf height. Holding the drill at an angle, drill through the top of the corbel and into the wall in two or more places. To secure the lower end of the corbel, use an awl to make a pilot hole in an inconspicuous spot. Nail the corbel to the wall.

4 Center the shelf over the corbels. Nail or screw the shelf to the corbel tops. Countersink the nails or screws. Fill all nail holes and retouch the paint. If desired, seal the shelf and corbels with polyurethane.

Everyday clothespins give this little table a look that's as pure and simple as laundry waving in the breeze. Often used on old **folk art** pieces, clothespins are an easy and inexpensive way to add decoration to an otherwise plain piece.

Bedside Table

Materials
- Small plain-lined table (new or unfinished); the one shown measures 26 inches tall and 12×17 inches at the top
- White acrylic or latex paint
- Peg-style clothes pins (90 to 100 for the size table shown)
- Drill with a small bit
- Wood glue
- 1¼-inch (#17) brads

Instructions
1 Paint the table and clothespins white. Inspect the clothespins for flaws before painting. Paint more than you anticipate needing as some will split when nailed.

2 Determine the number of clothespins needed to extend across each side of the table. You may need to leave a small space between each one so they fit evenly. Drill a small hole through each clothespin at precisely the same spot. The head of the clothespin should fall just above the tabletop.

3 Starting at one corner, place a dot of glue on the back of the clothespin. Slip a brad through the hole and pound it into the table edge. Place another clothespin at the opposite corner of the same side. Working toward the center, repeat until the edge is covered with clothespins. Repeat for the remaining sides of the table.

4 Fill the nail holes and retouch the paint.

Tufted Tuffet

Materials

- Purchased rectangular wooden tuffet
- Paint
- 2-inch-thick foam to fit the tuffet top
- Quilt batting
- Muslin
- Staple gun and staples
- Decorator fabric
- Upholstery fringe
- Screw-type upholstery tacks
- Hot-glue gun and glue sticks

Instructions

1 Paint the tuffet to coordinate with the decorator fabric.

2 Place the foam over the tuffet top. Lay the quilt batting and muslin over the foam, letting both drape over the sides several inches. Working from opposite sides, stretch the muslin tightly and staple it to the side of the stool top. Start stapling at the center and work toward the edges. Make sure the cover is smooth and even. Trim away the excess muslin and batting.

3 Cover the tuffet with the decorator fabric, making small inverted tucks at each corner. Staple the fabric in place and trim the excess so none hangs below the edge of the tuffet.

4 To tuft the top and sides, twist the upholstery tacks into the tuffet top. Hot-glue upholstery fringe over the staples at the edge of the tuffet, turning under the raw edge.

Upholstery fringe and tacks update a traditional wooden tuffet. Screw-type tacks are still available in decorator departments of fabric stores and at upholstery shops. Or seek out *vintage* tacks at flea markets and antiques shops.

Dangling points with jingle-bell tips add

Jester Points

Materials

- Purchased oval-shape wooden tuffet
- 2-inch-thick upholstery foam to fit the tuffet top
- Quilt batting
- Muslin
- Staple gun and staples
- Decorator fabric for the top and half the points
- Coordinating decorator fabric for the remaining points
- Upholstery braid
- Multicolor cording
- Small jingle bells

Instructions

1 Place the foam over the top. Cover the foam with batting and muslin, letting both drape several inches over the sides. Working from opposite sides, stretch the muslin tightly and staple it to the underside of the stool top. Place staples 1 to 2 inches apart and about 1 inch from the outside edge of the top.

Make sure the cover is smooth and even. Trim away the excess foam and batting.

2 Cover the tuffet with decorator fabric in the same manner.

3 To make the point pattern, draw a 4½-inch line on paper. Bisect it with a 5-inch line, forming a T. Join the ends to make a triangle. Add ¼ inch seam allowances. Cut 10 plain and 10 print triangles. (*Note:* The number of triangles may vary with the size of the tuffet.) With right sides facing, join the triangles in pairs, leaving an opening for turning. Turn, press, and slipstitch the opening closed. Trim ½ inch from the upper edge of the plain triangles to make them shorter.

4 Staple the triangles to the edge of the bench, slightly overlapping them. Glue braid over the raw edges, then glue cord over the braid. Sew a jingle bell to each point.

A short, **flirty** skirt gives a formal look to a plain bench. Use a lightweight fabric that gathers easily for the skirt. A heavier fabric with a tight weave works better for the tufted top. Finish it off with a grid of upholstery braid.

Mini-Skirted Stool

Materials

- Purchased oval-shape wooden tuffet
- 2-inch-thick foam to fit the tuffet top
- Quilt batting
- Muslin
- Staple gun and staples
- Decorator fabrics for the top and skirt
- Upholstery braid
- Fabric glue
- Hot-glue gun and glue sticks
- Screw-type upholstery buttons

Instructions

1 Place the foam over the tuffet top. Cover the foam with batting and muslin, letting both drape several inches over the sides. Working from opposite sides, stretch the muslin tightly and staple it to the underside of the stool top. Place staples 1 to 2 inches apart and about 1 inch from the outside edge of the top. Make sure the cover is smooth and even. Trim away the excess foam and batting.

2 Cover the tuffet with decorator fabric in the same manner. Pin two rows of braid diagonally across the top, spacing them evenly. Pin two additional rows of braid in the opposite direction, forming a grid. Glue the braid in place with fabric glue.

3 Cut the skirt fabric twice the circumference of the stool and double the desired depth. Stitch the short ends together. Fold the skirt in half lengthwise, wrong sides facing. Press the skirt and baste the top raw edges together. Finger-pleat the skirt to fit the tuffet, pinning the pleats in place. The pleats can be slightly uneven. Staple the skirt to the edge of the tuffet top. Hot-glue braid to the edge, covering the raw edges and staples.

4 To tuft the stool top, place a screw-type upholstery button at each braid intersection.

Draped and Tied

Materials

- Purchased rectangular wooden tuffet or existing padded tuffet
- 2-inch-thick foam to fit the tuffet top
- Quilt batting
- Muslin
- Staple gun and staples
- Decorator fabric
- Upholstery cord
- Fabric glue
- Liquid ravel preventer

Instructions

1 If you are using a new stool, pad the top as described for the Mini-Skirted Stool (step 1) on *page 44*. To make the cover, measure from the floor, up the side and across the top, and back to the floor in both directions. Add 1½ inches for hems. Cut a rectangle of fabric this size, slightly rounding the corners. Make all the corners the same shape.

2 Lay the cover over the stool and make any adjustments. Turn under the raw edges ¼ inch, then ½ inch and topstitch the hem in place. Place the cover over the stool so it sits on the top evenly.

3 Cut cording to fit each side, allowing several inches for a knot on each end. Pin the cording in place and tie the knots. Use small dots of fabric glue to secure the cord and knots. Trim the cord ends and seal them with liquid ravel preventer.

Pad a new unfinished stool or give an old bench a new look without having to strip away the original cover. Simply drape fabric over a padded tuffet, then tie it in place with cording.

Sometimes the easiest decorating *ideas* are hiding in the most unusual places. Open your eyes—and your mind—to table and storage possibilities just waiting to be **discovered**.

Step Up In Style

An old ladder stands up to the task as an end table with a new coat of paint and some graphic elements. For a more rustic look, skip the paint and just give the ladder a good cleaning. Here a small step stool is used for books, but taller ladders can be put to work holding plants and small collectibles.

It's Finial

This table straddles the line between modern sculpture and function. Simply paint and sand four large landscape finials (available at home improvement centers), then top them with a glass tabletop. Have the glass custom-cut or look for pre-cut shapes at decorating centers.

Getting Benched

In small spaces, substitute long, narrow benches for cumbersome coffee tables. Wash benches, step stools, and bench seats often can be found in garages, warehouses, and flea markets. Stack several together for a graphic effect.

A Case for Storage

If the perfect end table is nowhere to be found, head to the flea market and seek out old suitcases. Reproductions are also available in decorating and discount stores. For a bonus, use the extra storage space by filling the suitcases with seldom-used items.

ideas

bed and bath

Decorating is about making your home comfortable for your family,

and comfort *is key for bedrooms and baths.*

Start with plump pillows, cozy blankets,

and soft cotton towels, then add your own style.

Easy *custom headboards,*

bright bold bedding, and little touches of luxury *turn these*

rooms into special retreats.

Drape a Quilt

Materials
- Wooden drapery rod with finials
- Rod brackets and mounting hardware
- Quilt
- Brass quilters' safety pins

Instructions

1 Cut the drapery rod slightly longer than the width of the bed. Attach a finial to each end. Install the brackets according to the package directions and hang the rod.

2 Fold the quilt to take advantage of the best colors and patterns. Drape the quilt over the rod. To keep the quilt from shifting, pin both sides of the quilt together directly under the rod. Use brass quilters' pins (they will not rust or stain the fabric) and conceal them within the folds and layers of the fabric.

When a quilt is too small, too fragile, or too worn to use on the bed, turn it into a headboard instead. This option adds the same homespun feel to a room with splashes of pattern and color while reducing wear and tear on an antique **piece. To preserve a valuable quilt, keep it out of direct sunlight and periodically refold it in different directions to prevent creases and light damage.**

head

board

PVC pipe forms a sleek, lightweight frame for a tent-like **canopy** that highlights both a bed and window. The canopy is cut from two twin-size sheets and simply drapes over the pipes.

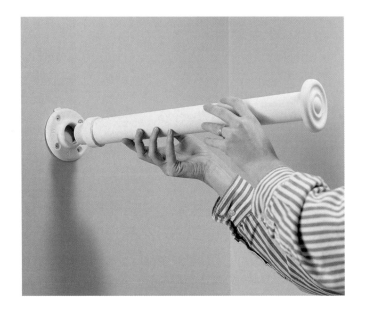

Pipe Dreams

Materials

- Three 18-inch lengths of white PVC pipe
- 3 threaded plugs to fit the pipes
- 3 white metal flanges to fit the plugs
- 3 caps for the pipes
- Screws
- Glue for PVC pipe
- 3 decorative wooden rosettes
- White paint
- 2 twin bed sheets

Instructions

1 On the wall, mark a point over the center of the bed near the ceiling. Mark a point on each side of the bed for the side brackets. Be sure to allow enough room for the bedding. Screw a flange to the wall at each point.

2 Paint the rosettes white. If necessary, paint any of the PVC pieces white.

3 Glue a threaded plug to one end of each pipe. Place a cap on the other end and glue a rosette to the cap. Screw the pipe into the flange. See the photograph *at left* for details.

4 For the canopy, measure from the floor, over all three pipes, and back to the floor. Cut each sheet into a 19-inch-wide strip equal to this measurement, piecing the strips as needed to achieve the proper length.

5 With right sides facing, sew the strips together using ½-inch seam allowances. Leave an opening for turning. Turn the strip, press, and slipstitch the opening closed. Drape the canopy panel over the brackets.

Old ceiling tins continue to crop up at flea markets, architectural salvage stores, and antiques shops. For an instant headboard, nail a row of tins to the wall. If large **salvage** matching tins aren't available, use rows of smaller or mismatched panels. Reproduction tins are also available at many home improvement centers.

Tin Tile Headboard

Materials

- Vintage or reproduction ceiling tins slightly larger than the width of the bed
- Drill with a small bit suitable for metal
- Awl
- Small flat-head nails

Instructions

1 Drill a small hole in each outer corner of each ceiling tin. If the tins are warped or large, drill additional holes along the outer edges of the tiles to secure them to the wall.

2 Holding the tins in place, mark through the holes and onto the wall. Remove the tins and use the awl to make a pilot hole at each mark. Nail the tins to the wall.

Padded with Pillows

Materials

- Wooden drapery rod with finials
- Rod brackets and mounting hardware
- Pillows to fit the width of the bed
- Purchased or handmade pillow shams
- 1-inch-wide ribbon or 2½-inch-wide fabric strips to match the shams

Instructions

1 Use either ribbon or fabric strips for hanging the pillows from the rod. To make fabric hangers, fold the fabric strips in half lengthwise with right sides facing. Using a ¼-inch seam allowance, sew along the long edges. Turn the strips to the right side and press.

2 Measure the depth of the flange on the sham. Double this and add 1 inch for the length of the hanging strip. Cut two strips for each Euro-sham (more for larger pillows.) Narrowly hem the raw edges. Shape each strip into a loop and sew across the short ends, overlapping the ends ½ inch. Tack the loops to the shams at the base of the flange.

3 Hold the pillows to the wall and mark the position of the rod. Cut the rod slightly longer than the width of the bed and attach the finials. Install the brackets according to the manufacturer's directions.

4 Slide the pillow loops onto the rod and lay the rod in place. Adjust the pillows.

Never again will your pillows droop and flop when you read in bed. Large square pillows hung from a drapery rod offer plenty of padding and a splash of color too. Use purchased oversized squares (called Euro-shams) or a row of king-size or body pillows.

Preassembled stockade fencing makes this garden-fresh headboard a breeze. Most home improvement stores will make any necessary cuts for a minimal charge. For stability, anchor the fence to the wall instead of the bed.

Picket Fences

Materials

- Preassembled stockade fencing
- Sandpaper
- Latex primer and paint
- Drywall screws, anchor bolts, or other appropriate fasteners

Instructions

1 Measure the width of the bed and the desired height. Have the fencing cut to size or cut it yourself. Sand the surfaces and wipe them clean, then paint and prime the fencing.

2 Stand the fencing in place. Using drywall screws, anchor bolts, or other appropriate fasteners, attach the fence to the wall at several points on each side. Slide the bed against the fence.

3 For a bed that sits in a corner at an angle, it may be necessary to cut triangular blocks of scrap 1×2 or 2×4 for braces. Attach the blocks to the wall, then attach the fence to the blocks. Use several blocks on each side to make sure the headboard is stable.

Painted Headboard

Materials
- Paper drop cloth
- Stencil plastic
- Crafts knife
- Low-tack painters' tape
- Spray stencil adhesive (optional)
- Stencil brushes
- Acrylic and latex paints in the desired colors
- Textile medium for acrylic paint

Instructions

1 Enlarge the headboard pattern *below* to the desired size. Cut the paper drop cloth larger than the finished pattern and fold it in half. Transfer the pattern to the paper, placing the long straight edge on the fold. Cut out the pattern, leaving a headboard-shaped window in the center of the paper. Open out the pattern and tape it to the wall in the desired position. If desired, apply stencil adhesive.

2 Tape the cut edge of the pattern to the wall, following the curves and angles. Trim the tape with a crafts knife to keep the lines even. Paint the headboard shape with two or more coats of the desired color (see the photograph *above*). Remove the pattern and tape. Touch up any rough edges.

3 For the wall and linen stencil, enlarge the daisy pattern *at left* to scale and cut it from stencil plastic. To stencil the wall, hold the stencil to the wall with tape or stencil adhesive. Dip the tip of the stencil brush in the paint, then tap it onto a paper plate to remove most of the paint. Pounce the brush through the stencil openings. Reload the brush and repeat the process until the entire wall is stenciled.

4 Using the wall color, stencil a single flower onto the headboard as shown *opposite*.

5 To stencil the linens, mix the acrylic paint with textile medium according to the manufacturer's directions. Place cardboard under the area to be stenciled and tape or weight the fabric so it is smooth and taut. Stencil the linens in the same manner as you stenciled the walls. Heat-set the paint according to the manufacturer's directions.

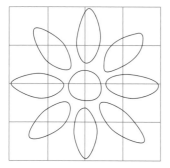

1 SQUARE = 1 INCH

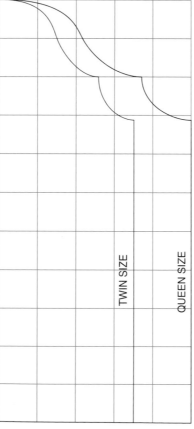

TWIN SIZE

QUEEN SIZE

1 SQUARE = 6 INCHES

Brush up on your painting skills with a headboard-shape wall pattern. Even linens make a statement with painted designs. Paint the tall, elegant headboard shape directly onto the wall, then scatter stenciled daisies on the remaining wall surface.

daisies

Fabric Frame

Materials

- Pre-stretched artist's canvas or canvases to fit the width of the bed
- Decorator fabric
- Staple gun and staples
- Coordinating gimp or ribbon

Instructions

1 Cut the fabric 3 inches larger on all sides than the canvas frame. If the fabric has a defined pattern, position it on the canvas to center the design.

2 Lay out the fabric, wrong side up. Center the canvas facedown over the fabric. Wrap the fabric to the back and staple it at the center of each side (see the photograph *below left* for details). The fabric should be taut, but not distorted. The canvas will give it extra body and make it less sheer. Working from the center staple to the outer edges, finish stapling one side. Repeat for the opposite side, then the remaining two sides. Fold the corners and trim away excess fabric to keep the back smooth and flat.

3 Beginning at the bottom of the canvas, glue gimp or ribbon around the sides (see the photograph *below right*).

4 Mark the position of the canvas just above the mattress. Hammer finish nails into the wall. Rest the inside of the frame on the nails.

Bring an **artistic** look to your bedroom without lifting a paintbrush. Fabric stretched over blank artist's canvas frames the bed with color and pattern. Cover one or more pre-stretched canvases with decorative fabric, then hang them just above the mattress.

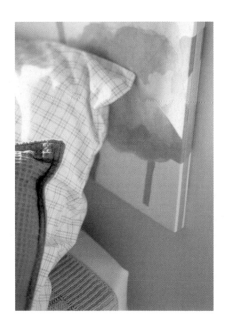

Take one plain duvet cover and a couple and loads of color,

and the result is an eye-popping bedding ensemble. Look for 100-percent-cotton linens with a flat, tight weave for the best results. If a plain *duvet* cover is not readily available, make one from two flat bedsheets cut to the size.

Painted Bed Linens

Materials
- Flat-finish white cotton duvet cover (purchased or self-made)
- 2 white square cotton Euro-shams
- Standard white cotton pillow sham
- Kraft paper
- Low-tack painter's tape
- Hard lead pencil
- Acrylic paints in the desired colors
- Textile medium to match the acrylic paints
- Textile paintbrushes

Instructions
Wash and dry all linens, then press them to remove all wrinkles. Do not use fabric softener, detergent with fabric softener or stain-repellent, or spray starch. These will prevent the paint from adhering.

For the duvet cover:

1 Lay the duvet cover on a large work surface or clean floor. Place kraft paper between the layers of fabric to prevent paint from bleeding through. Using painter's tape, fasten the duvet edges to the work surface so the fabric is smooth and taut, but not distorted.

2 Measure the duvet cover and divide it into squares, allowing 2½ inches between squares and around the edges for a border. Make a paper or cardboard template for the square pattern. Lightly draw the squares onto the duvet cover with a hard lead pencil.

3 Make templates for three different designs. The duvet cover shown *opposite* uses three simplified leaf patterns, but shapes from other designs in the room also could be used. Simplify all the designs so the patterns are bold and graphic.

4 On scrap paper, sketch a plan of the duvet and mark which designs will go into which squares. Leave some squares blank. Mark the color for each square. For the patterned squares, use the same color combination each time you repeat the pattern. For example, the fingerlike leaf *opposite* is always olive green and the background is always purple. Using the plan as your guide, trace the patterns onto the corresponding squares on the duvet. Lightly mark each square with the appropriate color name.

5 Mix the paints with textile medium according to the manufacturer's instructions. Brands vary, so be sure the paint and textile medium are compatible. Follow the instructions exactly.

6 Starting with one pattern, paint all of the designs in the squares containing that pattern. Repeat for the remaining patterns. Working with one color at a time, paint the corresponding backgrounds, leaving a ¼-inch margin of white between the pattern and the background.

7 Paint the remaining (unpatterned) squares. Paint the bands between the squares, leaving a ¼-inch margin of white between the squares and the bands. Let all the paint dry.

# of shams, add graphic designs

8 Using a narrow paintbrush, outline the designs and the squares with contrasting colors, filling in the ¼-inch margins of white. Let the paint dry.

9 Heat-set the duvet cover according to the textile medium and paint directions, or have a commercial laundry heat-set the colors. (Tell the laundry that the paint is unset and give them instructions for heat-setting.)

10 To launder the duvet cover, turn it inside out and follow laundering instructions on the paint and textile medium bottles. If no instructions are provided, use cool water and regular detergent. Tumble dry low. Press from the wrong side if necessary.

For the pillow shams:

1 Modify the designs to fit the shams (see the photograph *below* for details). Enlarge, reduce, or adapt dimensions to fit the pillow size and shape.

2 Paint, heat-set, and care for the shams in the same manner as the duvet cover.

Bamboo, sisal, coir, and other natural fiber rugs add a fresh look to floors. Add character to these inexpensive floor covers with a stenciled design. Here a fern frond is randomly scattered across the floor, changing directions for a casual appearance. Cut a stencil from our pattern or use a commercial pre-cut stencil.

Instructions

1 Enlarge the pattern *below* and cut it from stencil plastic. To determine design placement, cut sheets of paper to the approximate size and shape of the stencil. Scatter the shapes on the rug, adjusting the spacing as necessary.

2 Starting at the center of the rug, stencil the designs directly onto the rug. Tape the stencil to the rug. Dip the tip of the stencil brush in the paint. Tap the brush onto a paper plate until most of the paint is removed. Using a pouncing motion, pounce the paint through the stencil openings and into the rug fibers. Remove the stencil and tape and move to the next position. Repeat until all the designs are stenciled. Because of the texture of the rug, the painting will be uneven.

3 Let the paint dry completely. Apply one or two coats of polyurethane to the entire rug.

1 square = 1 inch

Skirted Sink

Materials

- Measuring tape
- Decorator fabric
- Light- to medium-weight drapery lining fabric
- ¼-inch diameter welt
- Monofilament
- Hook-and-loop fastening tape with one self-adhesive side and one sewable side

Instructions

Note: The skirt can be applied to the underside of the sink as shown or to the outside rim.

1 Measure the sink perimeter, omitting the width of the plumbing side. If the sink sits flush against the wall and the skirt will be applied to the outside of the sink, measure only to the wall on each side. Multiply the perimeter by 2½. For the length, measure from the sink bottom to the floor and add ½ inch. Cut the decorator and lining fabrics to these measurements, piecing as needed.

2 With right sides facing and raw edges aligned, baste the welt to the bottom of the skirt. Place the lining over the decorator fabric with right sides together and the welt sandwiched in between. Using a zipper foot, sew along the bottom edge close to the welt. Switch to a regular foot and sew the side seams, using a ½-inch seam allowance. Clip the corners, turn the skirt to the right side, and press.

3 Align the top raw edges and baste them together. Clean-finish the upper edges. Lay monofilament over the stitching line. Using a wide, long stitch, zigzag over the monofilament, taking care not to catch it in the stitching. Pull up the monofilament to gather the upper edge.

Dress up a purely functional sink and turn it into the focal point of a small powder room. The skirt not only adds charm, but also hides plumbing and provides hidden storage space. Self-adhesive hook-and-loop tape is the secret here, allowing the skirt to be removed easily for cleaning.

4 Cut a 4-inch-wide band to match the finished skirt width. Press one long edge under ½ inch. With right sides facing and raw edges aligned, pin the band to the lining side of the skirt. Adjust the gathers so the skirt fits the band and the band seam allowances extend beyond the skirt edge on both ends. Baste the band to the skirt.

5 Fold the band in half lengthwise, right sides facing. Sew across the short edges. Turn the band to the right side and over the top of the skirt top, encasing the raw edges. Topstitch the folded edge of the band in place over the top edge and the gathering.

6 Attach the adhesive-backed side of the hook-and-loop tape to the inside edge of the sink. Sew the remaining portion of the hook-and-loop tape to the decorative side of the skirt band. Beginning at the center and working out, hang the skirt by pressing the two halves of the hook-and-loop tape together. To place the skirt on the outside of the sink, apply the adhesive hook-and-loop tape to the outside of the sink and the sewable side of the tape to the band lining.

Ribbon Stripes

Materials
- Solid-color towel with a woven band insert
- Measuring tape
- Cotton fabric for the stripe base
- Pieces of washable ribbon in a variety of widths and colors

Instructions

1 Wrap the ribbons into loose coils and secure each coil with a scrap of the same ribbon. Place the ribbons in a mesh lingerie laundry bag and launder them to prevent shrinkage and bleeding when the towels are washed and dried.

2 Measure the width of the towel and add 1 inch. Measure the depth of the woven band and add 1 inch. Cut a cotton strip to these dimensions. If you are trimming more than one towel, make one large strip that is equal to the band size for the total number of towels and as wide as the widest towel plus 1 inch. For example, if each towel has a band 1½ inches deep, the strip size for each towel

Let plain bath towels earn their stripes with a *patchwork* of washable ribbons. Sew odd-lot pieces of ribbon together, then stitch them onto the towels for multicolored stripes. For a completely coordinated look, use the same treatment on hand towels, rugs, shower curtains, and window treatments.

is 2½ inches deep (1½ inches plus 1 inch for seam allowances). For three towels, cut a strip 7½ inches deep (3×2½ inches) and 1 inch wider than the widest towel.

3 Arrange ribbons side-by-side on the cotton strip, overlapping the ribbons slightly to completely cover the strip. Topstitch the ribbons along the overlapped edges.

4 For multiple towels, cut the large strip into individual ones, cutting across the stitched edges of the ribbons. Press all edges of the strip under ½ inch. Pin the strip over the woven band on the towel and topstitch along all edges.

finishing touches

It's the little things in life—and decorating—that count.

Details such as custom-made pillows, lampshades trimmed with

ribbons or flowers, well-framed pictures, and creative

display spaces take a room

from functional to fantastic.

Fit to Be Tied

Materials

- 2 cloth dinner napkins
- Purchased pillow the same size or slightly smaller than the napkins
- 4⅔ yards of ⅝-inch-wide double-faced satin ribbon

Instructions

1 Cut the ribbon into 7-inch lengths. Tack a ribbon 2 inches from each corner and at the center of the front napkin. There will be a total of 12 ribbons tacked to this napkin. Repeat for the back napkin.

2 Sandwich the pillow between the napkins and tie the ribbons to hold the cover in place.

Whip up pillow **covers** in an hour or less. Inexpensive cloth napkins come in standard sizes, have hemmed edges, and are available in almost unlimited and patterns. They make a perfect case for turning plain pillows into *bold* statements. For one of the simplest treatments (see the top of the stack *opposite*), tack ribbons to the corners and sides of two napkins, then tie the cloths over a purchased pillow.

Some napkins come with small openings as a part of their decorative trim. Often called openwork or cutwork, these bands of open spaces are perfect for sashing two napkins into a cover. The open band is often inset between an outer border and the body of the napkin, forming a flat, flanged edge.

Do the Weave

Materials

- 2 cloth dinner napkins with a band of even openwork along the edges
- Purchased pillow slightly smaller than the center portion of the napkins (inside the openwork)
- Narrow cording (3 yards for a 20-inch napkin)
- Clear fabric glue

Instructions

1 Dip the ends of the cording into the fabric glue and let them dry. The glue will keep the ends from fraying and provide a stiff end for lacing through the openwork.

2 Line up the napkins, wrong sides facing, so the holes match. Starting at one corner, lace the cording through the holes at 1-inch intervals on three sides of the cover.

3 Slip the pillow into the cover. Continue lacing until the pillow is closed. Adjust the cording as needed and tie the ends in a bow. Trim the ends of the bow and place a small dot of glue on each end to prevent fraying. *Note:* Because the center of the pillow is stuffed and the edges are flat, the flanges may pucker slightly.

Buttoned-Down Accent

- Purchased plain pillow or two cloth dinner napkins and a pillow form to fit
- Cloth cocktail napkin
- 4 matching buttons

1 To cover a pillow form with plain napkins, place the napkins wrong sides together and topstitch along three edges close to the hem. Slip the pillow form inside, push it away from the open edge, and pin the opening closed. Topstitch the remaining edge closed, taking care not to catch the pillow form. Fluff the pillow to distribute the form evenly.

2 Make a buttonhole in each corner of the cocktail napkin. Center the cocktail napkin over the pillow and mark the position of the buttonholes. Remove the cocktail napkin and sew a button at each mark.

3 Button the cocktail napkin in place. To make a seasonal topper, replace the cocktail napkin with one that has a holiday or seasonal motif.

Add a dash of color and pattern by buttoning a cocktail napkin over a plain pillow. Use a purchased pillow or cover a pillow form with plain dinner napkins. If you keep the button color neutral or match it to the pillow, you'll be able to switch the cocktail napkin for holidays or a change of seasons.

Zippity-Quick Cover

Materials
- 2 plain linen napkins
- Contrasting zipper longer than the napkins
- Pillow form the same size as the napkins

Instructions

1 Fold one napkin in half and lightly press it along the fold. Cut along the crease. Press under ⅛ inch on each raw edge. (These halves will be the pillow front.)

2 Pin the pressed edges of the napkin halves to the zipper, leaving the teeth exposed and a ¼-inch gap between the pressed edges. The zipper should extend beyond the napkin on both ends. Fold each end back to the wrong side of the napkin.

3 Using a zipper foot, sew along the pressed edges to attach the napkin halves to the zipper. Unzip the zipper so the head is toward the center of the napkin.

4 Place the front and back napkins together, wrong sides facing. Edgestitch along all four edges. Insert the pillow form and zip the cover closed.

A *zipper* of a contrasting color becomes the focal point for a solid-color, textural linen napkin. If you want to further emphasize the zipper, loop a small tassel through the tab or attach a *charm* using a split ring. For an even funkier look, place the zipper off-center.

Lashed Edging

Materials

- 2 cloth dinner napkins
- Purchased pillow the same size or slightly smaller than the napkins
- Forty ½-inch grommets and grommet tool
- Cording to fit the grommets (3 yards for a 20-inch pillow)
- Liquid ravel preventer or clear fabric glue

Instructions

1 Following the manufacturer's instructions, install a grommet 2 inches from each corner of the top napkin. Evenly space 3 additional grommets along each side. Repeat for the back napkin.

2 Align the two napkins, wrong sides facing. Starting at one corner, lace three sides together through the grommets. If the cord bunches and frays when going through the grommets, wrap tape over the end to stiffen it for lacing.

3 Insert the pillow form and finish lacing. Tie the ends in a knot or bow. Trim the ends and treat them with liquid ravel preventer or clear fabric glue.

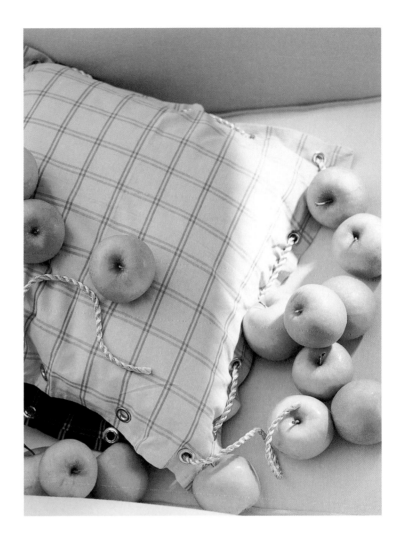

Hardware is hot, so give your pillow cover a trendy look with oversized grommets and chunky lacing. Use two matching napkins for the cover, or mix and match them for a reversible option.

Memory Wall

Materials

- Old frames of similar sizes but different shapes
- White spray paint
- White mat boards
- Vintage photographs
- Butcher or kraft paper
- Low-tack painter's tape

Instructions

1 Trace each frame onto paper. Cut out the templates and set them aside.

2 Paint all the frames with two or more coats of white paint. Place the photographs in the frames, using white mats.

3 To determine the positions of the frames, arrange the paper templates on the floor. Align the bottom edges of some frames with the top edges of others, align some left- or right-hand edges, and center some frames over others.

4 When you are pleased with the arrangement, tape the templates to the wall, adjusting the alignments as needed. Working with one frame at a time, replace the paper template with a framed photograph.

Turn chaos into a **collage** of memories with coordinating frames and mats. Choose frames from the same general era, then paint them all one color. Use matching mats for all the photos to place further emphasis on what's inside. Once you have framed and matted all the photographs, plot out your arrangement with paper templates.

Don't regret growing older.
It is a priviledge denied by many.
Anonymous

Make it a rule never to regret and never to look back.
Marjorie Kinnan Rawlings

No great artist ever sees things as they really are.
If he did, he would cease to be an artist.
Oscar Wilde

Make subtle, tasteful statements by framing your favorite quotes. If lettering isn't one of your talents, use attractive computer fonts to spell out the sayings. Matching frames and wide mats will draw attention to your wise **words.**

Post Your Quotes

Materials

- Black hand-lettered or computer-generated quotations on white paper
- Matching narrow black frames
- White mat board cut to fit each quote and frame

Instructions

1 Hand-letter or print the quotations. Use the same lettering style or typeface and size for all the pieces. The length of the quotation and number of lines can vary.

2 Mat and frame each of the pieces. If you don't want to cut the mats yourself, take them to a frame shop.

3 Hang the frames so they align perfectly, leaving about 1 inch between them.

Note: To keep down the cost, purchase standard-size frames, then fit the quotes and mats to the frames. This eliminates the expense of custom framing.

tone

Decorate a wall with a gallery of photos that you can change as easily as tying a bow. For a clean look, keep the frames simple and identical; add pattern and color by gluing fabric to pre-cut mats. To unify a variety of photos, have a professional photo processor convert them to sepia-tone prints.

Photo Gallery

Materials

- Photographs with a similar theme
- Purchased or self-cut mat boards
- Coordinating fabric
- Tacky white glue or fabric glue
- Disposable foam brush
- Matching frames
- Screw eyes
- Drapery rod and hanging hardware
- Ribbon for hanging pictures

Instructions

1 Check your local phone directory for a professional photo processor who works in sepia tones and does custom coloring. If any photographs are in color, have black and white prints made from the negatives. Then have the processor make sepia duplicates, adjusting the color to the desired tint. You can ask to have photographs cropped, reduced, or enlarged at the same time, if you wish. The photographs *at right* illustrate the color change.

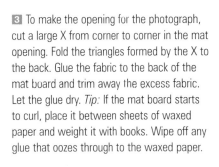

2 Position the fabric over the mat board. Cut the fabric 2 inches larger than the mat board on all sides. Lightly spread glue over the front of the mat board and smooth the fabric in place. Wrap the fabric to the back, mitering the corners, and glue it in place.

3 To make the opening for the photograph, cut a large X from corner to corner in the mat opening. Fold the triangles formed by the X to the back. Glue the fabric to the back of the mat board and trim away the excess fabric. Let the glue dry. *Tip:* If the mat board starts to curl, place it between sheets of waxed paper and weight it with books. Wipe off any glue that oozes through to the waxed paper.

4 Place the photos and mats in the frames. Place screw eyes on the back of each frame near the top. Loop ribbon through the screw eyes. Following the manufacturer's directions, hang a drapery rod on the wall where the photographs will be displayed. Tie the ribbons around the rod so the pictures hang at different heights.

Framing Hardware

- Old door hardware such as doorknobs, keys, knockers, and doorplates
- Old frames to fit the hardware
- Foam-core board to fit the frames
- Decorative paper to match the hardware
- Sandpaper (optional)
- Spray adhesive
- Heavy-duty adhesive for metal

Don't knock this display. Old door parts with elaborate detailing deserve a place of *honor* **in a collector's home. Mount the hardware against decorative papers, then surround it with a frame that reflects the style of the** hardware.

Instructions

1 If necessary, sand, paint, or otherwise finish the frames to blend with the hardware. If the pattern in the decorative paper is too strong, lightly sand the paper.

2 Trim the paper to fit the foam-core board and glue it to the board with spray adhesive. Place the foam-core board in the frame.

3 Glue keys, doorplates, and other flat items to the foam-core board. For pieces with a shank, cut a small hole in the foam-core board to receive the shank. Slide the shank through the hole and glue the piece in place.

Plate Rail Display

Materials

- Wide crown molding
- 1×2 pine board
- Saw with miter capabilities
- L-shape brackets
- Small wood screws and finish nails
- Toggle bolts or similar fasteners
- Wood glue
- Paint
- Paintable wood filler

Instructions

1 Cut the molding to the desired length, mitering the ends with a 45-degree angle. Cut a piece for the end of each shelf, mitering the corners. This piece will determine the depth of the shelf. Glue and nail the ends to the front.

2 Rip the 1×2 to fit inside the molding frame, slightly below the top of the molding. This creates a small lip to keep the displayed items in place.

3 Paint the molding frame and the shelf. For a whitewashed finish like the one shown *opposite*, dilute white paint with water until it is the consistency of milk. Paint the molding and shelf, and then wipe away the excess paint before it dries. If needed, reapply the paint in the same manner until the desired finish is achieved.

4 Using a level, mark the position of the shelf on the wall. Attach the L-shape brackets to the wall with toggle bolts, placing them 1 inch below the marked line. The bracket should be upside down so the leg against the wall is pointing toward the floor and the other leg is parallel to the ceiling. Lay the shelf over the brackets and screw it in place from the underside.

5 Position the molding over the shelf, concealing the brackets. Nail the molding to the shelf. Countersink the nails, fill the holes, and retouch the paint.

display

If your room lacks a plate rail to **display** photographs or mementos, make your own from stock crown molding. Better yet, install a row of rails that showcase a roomful of photos in one small space. Frame and mat all the photographs in the same way for a unified, album-like look.

racks

Rack 'Em Up

Materials

- 1×8 pine board
- Stemware molding (available at home improvement centers)
- Paint
- Wood glue
- Screws and finish nails
- Paintable wood filler

Instructions

1 Enlarge the pattern *at right* to scale and cut two brackets for each shelf from the 1×8 board. Cut a 6×32-inch shelf for the small rack and a 7¼×48-inch shelf for the large rack. Position the brackets on the underside of the shelves, placing them 3 inches from each end and flush with the back. Glue, clamp, and nail them into place.

2 Cut the stemware molding into seven 5-inch pieces for the small shelf and eleven 6-inch pieces for the large shelf. From these pieces, cut one left and one right piece by removing the appropriate lip so the rail fits flush against the bracket (see the photograph *opposite* for detail.) Paint the shelves, brackets, and rails.

3 Glue and nail the right and left rails in place, flush with both the side brackets and the back of the shelf. Evenly space the remaining rails on the underside of the shelf, center-spacing them 3¾ inches apart. Glue and nail the pieces in place.

4 Mark a level line on the wall at the desired height. Drill at an angle through the top of the shelf and into the wall studs. Countersink the nails and screws, fill and sand the holes, and retouch the paint.

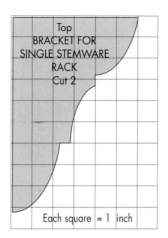

Top
BRACKET FOR
SINGLE STEMWARE
RACK
Cut 2

Each square = 1 inch

Stemware is safe and close at hand with these elegant and functional racks. Top each with a shelf for even more storage space. Rows of candles make the stemware sparkle.

Plates, photographs, or collectibles also would make a fine statement.

Such a Hutch

- Wallpaper and wallpaper hanging supplies
- 1×6 poplar ripped to 4 inches wide
- Standard windowsill stock
- Screen molding
- Quarter-round molding
- Colonial casing
- Chair rail
- Wood glue
- Screws and finish nails

Instructions

1 Draw the desired dimensions of the hutch onto the wall, and then wallpaper inside these lines. The bottom should be about 32 inches up from the floor.

2 *Note:* Paint all the wood pieces after cutting, but before assembling. Following the drawn dimensions, build the outer frame from the poplar strips. Cut windowsill stock for the shelves and nail the shelves to the frame, allowing enough space between each shelf to accommodate the pieces you plan to display.

Glue and tack a strip of screen molding onto the top of each windowsill piece 2½ inches from the back to form a lip that keeps the plates from sliding. Mount the box onto the wall by angling screws through the windowsill strips and into wall studs.

3 Cut the remaining moldings to fit the windowsill stock and paint each piece. See the photograph *at left* for details on the molding placement. Glue and nail colonial casing to the underside of each windowsill strip, aligning the back edges. Attach quarter-round to the front of the colonial molding with glue and nails as shown.

4 If you don't already have a chair rail in place, cut and paint lengths of chair rail molding to fit your walls. Mark a horizontal line even with the bottom of the plate rack and wallpaper to this line. Attach the chair rail to the wall at the rack base, covering the wallpaper edge. Fill all holes and retouch the paint.

Replicate a built-in hutch with one that is a single-plate deep. Windowsill, colonial casing, and other stock molding combine to make the faux shelf. Extending the

wallpaper behind the hutch furthers the illusion of depth.

Got Them Pegged

Materials

- 1×8 pine boards
- Decorative molding
- 2-inch-long Shaker pegs
- Drill with a bit to fit the Shaker pegs
- Paint
- Wood glue
- Screws and finish nails
- Paintable wood filler

Instructions

For the wall rail:

1 *Note:* Paint all the boards after cutting but before assembling. Cut the pine boards the length of the wall, butting them against window or door frames and into the corners. Rip the boards to 4 inches wide for the shelf and 3⅜ inches wide for the peg rails. Glue and nail the shelf to the rail with the back edges flush and at right angles.

2 Cut decorative molding to fit the joint between the shelf and the rail. Glue and nail the molding in place.

3 Drill holes to receive the pegs, spacing them approximately 5 inches apart and 1¼ inches from the bottom edge of the rail. Drill the holes just deep enough to receive the shank of the peg. Do not drill all the way through the board. Paint the pegs and set them aside.

4 With a level, mark where the top of the shelf will be placed. Using a countersink bit, drill through some of the peg holes to mount the rail to the wall. If possible, drill into studs.

5 Glue the pegs in place. Fill all holes and retouch the paint.

For the window pegs:

Note: The shelf attaches to the existing window frame from the top and the peg rack hangs from the shelf, covering the upper portion of the window frame. By hanging the unit this way, there is no visible damage to the original window frame.

1 Cut a pine board into a 2½-inch-wide peg rail and a 3¼-inch-wide shelf. Cut the peg rail long enough to fit over the upper window frame. Cut the shelf slightly longer than the peg rail.

2 Drill holes for the pegs in the peg rail in the same manner as step 3 for the wall rail.

3 Place the shelf along the top of the window frame and butt it against the wall. Mark a line on the underside of the shelf where the front edge of the window frame meets the underside of the shelf. Center the back edge of the peg rail along this line. A lip should extend to the back of the peg rail. This will attach to the upper edge of the window frame. The shelf should also extend to the front of the peg rail. Glue and nail the peg rail to the shelf. Paint the shelf, rail, and pegs.

4 Position the shelf on the top of the window frame and drive screws through the shelf and into the top of the window frame. Glue the pegs in place.

Shaker pegs ring this room at varying heights, acting as hangers for the curtains as well as photographs. Cap the peg rail with a shelf for even more display space. Purchased shaped Shaker pegs were used here, but you could substitute dowels for a more contemporary look.

Perky Patchwork

Materials

- Plain white chandelier shade
- Assorted calico fabrics
- Narrow rickrack
- Tacky white crafts glue
- Disposable foam brush

Instructions

1 Cut the fabrics into 1-inch squares. Cut enough squares to cover the shade, leaving a small amount of space between pieces.

2 Lightly brush the backs of the squares with tacky glue and press them onto the shade. Let the glue dry.

3 Cut a 5-inch piece of rickrack for each square. Glue the rickrack around the squares, folding it at three of the corners and overlapping the ends at the final corner. Trim away the excess rickrack.

Dress up a plain chandelier with well-trimmed shades. Combine different coordinating shades for a whimsical look, or keep them the same for classic style.

Plain paper or fabric shades make the best base for fabric, ribbon, painted, and stamped trims. Avoid glossy-finish shades. Some of the *decorations* may not adhere well to a slick surface.

On the Ball

Materials
- Plain white chandelier shade
- Ball fringe
- Hot-glue gun and glue sticks

Instructions

1 Cut the ball fringe strip 1 inch longer than the circumference of the lower edge of the shade.

2 Hot-glue the braid portion of the fringe to the lower edge of the shade so the balls hang below the rim. Turn under the raw edge at the end of the braid and glue it in place.

Take a trip back in time with swingy ball fringe. Fabric stores are lining their shelves with the groovy stuff once again and decorator shops carry multicolored fringe like that shown here.

If your tastes are more traditional than trendy, substitute any other upholstery fringe or braid for the ball fringe.

Rows of patterned ribbon band both the upper and lower edges of a quick-to-do shade.

ribbon

Look for dotted, striped, plaid, floral, ethnic, or holiday ribbons. Some even sport inserts of beads, mirrors, or woven patterns.

Avoid wide ribbons. When cut to fit the lower edge of a cone-shape shade, they may pucker at the upper edge.

Playing with the Bands

Materials
- Plain white chandelier shade
- Ribbon
- Hot-glue gun and glue sticks or thick white crafts glue

Instructions

1 Cut one piece of ribbon 1 inch longer than the circumference of the upper edge of the shade and another ribbon 1 inch longer than the circumference of the lower edge.

2 Glue the ribbon to the upper and lower edges of the shade. Turn the cut ends under to conceal the raw edge and overlap the beginning and ending edges by about ½ inch.

Paint circus-tent stripes all around a plain paper shade. Match the color to your walls or dilute it with a bit of white to create a lighter hue. Because the shade is wider at the bottom than at the top, the stripes will also be wider at the bottom and slightly triangular. The more cone-shaped the shade, the more triangular the painted portions will be.

Yipes, Stripes

Materials
- Plain white chandelier shade (a matte-finish paper shade works best)
- Low-tack painter's tape
- Rigid plastic card
- Acrylic paint
- Disposable foam brush

Instructions

1 Mask off stripes with low-tack painter's tape, spacing them evenly around the shade and wrapping the tape to the inside at the top and bottom edges. Seal the tape to the shade by running a rigid plastic card over the edges of the tape.

2 Paint the exposed areas with two or more coats of acrylic paint. When the paint dries, remove the tape.

Do the Twist

- Plain white chandelier shade
- Pencil and measuring tape
- ⅝-inch-wide grosgrain ribbon
- Hot-glue gun and glue sticks or thick white crafts glue

1 Divide the shade into even increments along both the top and bottom edges. Glue a strip of ribbon from one point to another, forming a diagonal line. Turn the ribbon to the inside at both the top and bottom edges.

2 Glue additional rows of ribbon parallel to the first strip.

Narrow grosgrain ribbon glued in a spiral pattern gives a simple but vibrant touch to this shade. To keep the spacing even, be sure to measure between each line of ribbon, making small pencil marks to use as a gluing guide.

Sticker Situation

Materials
- Plain white chandelier shade (matte-finish paper shade works best)
- Removable stickers in geometric shapes
- Rigid plastic card
- Acrylic paint

Instructions

1 Apply the stickers randomly over the shade. Seal the edges with a rigid plastic card so paint cannot seep under them.

2 Paint the shade with two or more coats of acrylic paint. Carefully remove the stickers after the paint dries.

Geometric shapes form a fun pattern when scattered across a shade. Removable stickers are the trick to making smooth, even shapes. Paint over the *stickers* and then remove them to reveal the unpainted portions of the shade. Because the paint is opaque, the shapes will have a slight glow when the light is turned on.

Seeing Spots

Materials

- Plain white chandelier shade (matte finish paper shade works best)
- Round pre-inked mini stamps in three colors

Instructions

1 Apply clusters of dots to the shade by lightly pressing each pre-inked stamp to the shade. Let some of the clusters extend beyond the upper and lower edges of the shade. Support the shade underneath with one hand and stamp with the other.

2 Let the ink dry completely. This may take several hours depending on the humidity, the shade surface, and how much ink was applied. Ink will not dry on a glossy shade and will smear when touched.

Pre-inked mini stamps are a hit with the kids. Find out just how much fun they are by stamping a shade with clusters of round dots. Choose three different colors that will coordinate with your room, then stamp away.

It doesn't take a green thumb to grow this garden. Plant some silk roses on a plain paper shade for a bloomin' great accent. The vase-shaped lamp base perfectly accommodates the flowery shade. If your roses are large and full, choose a shade one size smaller than you would ordinarily use on the lamp so the finished lamp won't look top heavy.

oses

Shade in Bloom

Materials
- Plain paper or fabric lampshade
- Silk roses and leaves in scale with the shade (large roses for a large shade, small rosebuds for a small shade)
- Heavy-duty shears or wire cutters
- High temperature hot-glue gun and glue sticks or epoxy

Instructions
1 Snip the roses and leaves from the stems. Glue two rows of leaves to the top and bottom edges of the shade, overlapping the leaves and letting them extend slightly beyond the shade.

2 Working from the bottom up, glue rows of roses to the remainder of the shade. Pack the roses tightly so very little shade shows.

Note: Hot glue (especially low-temperature glue) will soften at high temperatures, so this shade is best for lamps with low-watt bulbs. If the bulb is close to the shade, use epoxy to glue the roses in place, but be sure to let the epoxy set completely. Some epoxy adhesives are flammable when liquid, but are safe once the adhesive has hardened.

Shine a light on your own personal style by embellishing a standard lampshade. Start with a white, cream, or parchment shade and paint it to match your room. Then place stickers or clip-art designs on the shade to repeat the theme or motif of your decorating scheme.

Color It Yours

Materials

- Matte-finish paper shade
- Acrylic paint in the desired color and white
- Low-tack painter's tape
- Large flower stickers or clip-art designs (available in books at art supply and crafts stores)
- Decoupage medium

Instructions

1 Using long, even strokes, cover the shade with two or more coats of paint. For the yellow shade, after the paint dries, mask off the top and bottom 1½ inches of the shade. Mix equal parts of the main color with white and paint the top and bottom bands. After the paint dries, place it on the lighted lamp to check for streaks. Touch up as needed.

2 For the yellow shade, press stickers along the top and bottom edges. For the blue shade, photocopy and cut out clip-art images. Coat the backs of the cutouts with decoupage medium and smooth the images onto the shade. Let dry.

3 Finish either shade with two coats of decoupage medium. This coating will help hold the stickers or cutouts in place and make it easier to clean the shade.

Create your own designer candle shades by covering paper
shades (sometimes called candle chasers) with paper napkins.
Look for napkins with scalloped or shaped edges, a blend of
patterns, and bright, bold colors.

simple

Use Your Napkin

Materials

- Plain candle shade with follower hardware (available at crafts and decorating stores)
- Dinner-size decorative paper napkin
- Spray adhesive

Instructions

1 Drape the napkin over the shade. Mark the points where the napkin overlaps to create a straight seam. *Note:* The pattern may not align at this point. Mark the top edge of the shade.

2 Cut the napkin on the marked lines, adding ½-inch overlap at the seam. Spray the shade and napkin with adhesive following the manufacturer's directions. Smooth the napkin in place over the shade.

Note: Both permanent and repositionable spray adhesives are available at art supply stores. The repositionable adhesive allows you to adjust the napkin before the bond is tight; but because the napkin is thin, it may be difficult to remove once you've smoothed it into place.

Falling Leaves

Materials

- Matte-finish paper shade
- Wide low-tack painter's tape
- Leaf pattern or small leaf
- Lightweight cardboard
- Acrylic paint

Instructions

1 Draw or trace the leaf pattern or a small leaf onto lightweight cardboard and cut it out. Trace the pattern onto the nonadhesive side of low-tack painter's tape and cut out a large number of leaves.

2 Place the shade on a lighted lamp. Randomly apply the tape leaves to the shade. The light will help you space the leaves evenly. Remove the shade. Place one hand under a leaf to support the shade and seal the leaf to the shade using a rigid plastic card. Repeat for all leaves.

3 Using long, even strokes, paint the shade with two coats of acrylic paint. After the paint dries, place the shade on a lighted lamp to check for streaks. Touch up as needed.

4 Let the paint dry completely, then peel away the leaves. Place the shade on the lamp. When the light is turned on, the white leaves will glow slightly against the opaque painted background.

Leaves scattered over a paper shade bring the look of nature indoors. Draw your own leaf shape or copy one from a stencil, wallpaper, or gift wrap design; or trace real leaves. Cut the shapes from wide low-tack painter's tape and press them to the shade. Paint the shade to match your room, then remove the tape, and see the white leaves magically appear.

Shades of Elegance

For the corded lampshade:

Materials
- Plaster lamp with a paper shade
- Two or more closely related colors of acrylic paint
- Clean, lint-free rags
- Tape measure and pencil
- Narrow cording
- Glue-on studs
- Thick white crafts glue or epoxy

Instructions

1 Paint the lamp base with the lightest color of paint and let it dry. Using a damp rag that has been wrung dry, rub on the darker color paint, letting the base coat show through in places. If desired, apply a third color of paint.

2 Rub a small amount of paint onto the shade. Use the most prominent color from the base and rub it on lightly and unevenly.

3 Measure the top and bottom of the shade and divide both into even increments. Mark a point halfway between each bottom mark so there are twice as many points on the bottom as on the top.

4 Cut pieces of cord slightly longer than the depth of the shade. Glue one end of each cord to a mark at the top of the shade. Glue the remaining end to a point below the top mark. Glue all the cords in place, skipping every other point along the bottom edge.

5 After the glue dries, trim the cord even with the shade edge. Glue a stud over each end of every cord and at the intervening marked points.

For the seashell lamp and shade:

Materials
- Plaster candlestick-style lamp base
- Pastel, silver, and pearlescent spray paints
- Tiny sea shells (available at crafts and import stores)
- Thick white crafts glue
- Spray sealer
- Linen-textured lampshade
- Starfish (available at crafts and import stores)
- Hot-glue gun and glue sticks or epoxy

Instructions

1 Spray paint the lamp base with pastel paint. Highlight the base with a mist of both silver and pearlescent paint.

2 Lay the lamp on its side. Brush a thick coat of thick white crafts glue onto the neck of the lamp. Press small seashells into the glue, covering the neck. After the glue dries, turn the lamp and repeat. Repeat until the entire neck is covered with shells. Spray the base with sealer.

3 Glue starfish to the shade. Lightly mist the finished shade with a spray of both silver and pearlescent paint.

Rich textures make you want to reach out and Pebbly bases enhanced with paint and shades sporting studs, cords, and starfish catch the light in intriguing ways and beg you

extures

touch elegant lamps like these.

to take notice.

simply wonderful

windows

They're your view of the world, the *light* of your room, and sometimes

the biggest decorating challenge in your home. Deciding what

kind of window *treatment* to use isn't always easy.

On the following pages, you'll find ways to add *personality* by

embellishing ready-made draperies, adding indoor window boxes,

or capping a window with a valance.

Tall transom windows offer a long list of decorating dilemmas: where to hang the rod, how to let in the *light* yet preserve privacy, and even where to find draperies of the right length. Here's a simple solution: Add a sheer panel to the top of lightweight ready-made draperies, then hang the rod almost at ceiling height to fill the entire wall.

Sheer Delight

Materials
- Purchased lightweight, unlined drapery panel
- Sheer fabric for the top
- Wide upholstery cord with a lip or flange
- Narrow upholstery cord for top ties

Instructions

1 Cut the sheer fabric 30 inches long and the width of the drapery panel. Add ½ inch for a narrow hem at each short end. *Note:* Cutting the fabric so the crosswise grain runs up and down for the depth will eliminate piecing. Shorten the drapery panel from the top, cutting away the upper hem. Allow for a 26-inch sheer panel above the purchased panel, a ½-inch seam allowance, and enough length to let the drapery hang to the floor.

2 Hem the narrow ends of the sheer panel. On the top edge, press under ½ inch, then 3 inches. Topstitch along the folded edge to form the upper hem.

3 Baste the wide upholstery cord to the right side of the lower panel so the edge of the cord is along the seam allowance and the lip faces toward the raw edge of the drapery. Place the sheer panel over the lower panel, right sides facing, sandwiching the cord between the fabrics. Using a zipper foot and a ½-inch seam allowance, sew the panels together close to the cord. Open out the panels and press the seam allowances toward the lower panel.

4 For the hanging loops, at one edge make a pair of 1-inch-long vertical buttonholes, spacing them 1 inch apart. Evenly space additional pairs of buttonholes along the top edge of the panel, placing them about 12 inches apart.

5 Cut the narrow cord into 18-inch lengths. Knot one end. Thread the other end from front to back through the left buttonhole, over the rod, and from back to front through the right buttonhole. Knot the end. Tie the ends of the cord together, forming a small pleat. Repeat for each of the remaining buttonholes.

A few quick embellishments add pizzazz to a plain *piqué* panel. Daisy trims and ribbon ties are further enhanced by a stylish rod. Drawing the curtain to one side and letting it swag gives it a fresh, **updated** look.

Bright with Blooms

Materials

- Plain piqué or linen-like drapery panel wide enough to cover the entire window
- 1½-inch-wide washable sheer ribbon cut into 27-inch-long strips
- Large purchased ribbon daisies
- Fabric glue or needle and thread

Instructions

1 Press the rod pocket smooth so it becomes an upper hem. Fold the ribbons in half crosswise and sew the fold to the upper edge of the drapery panel. Start 1 inch from the edge and space the ribbons evenly across the top, placing them about 8 inches apart.

2 Glue or tack a daisy at the base of each ribbon, covering the stitching. If the curtains will be laundered often, tack the daisies so they can be removed for washing.

3 Tie the ribbons over the drapery rod. Because the ribbons add length, the rod may need to be hung higher than normal.

Knob Appeal

Materials

- 1×4 pine board slightly longer than the width of the window frame
- Doorknobs (enough to be spaced about 12 inches apart, plus 2 for tie-backs)
- Dowels to fit the doorknob shanks
- Countersink drill bit and drill
- Screws and bolts
- Wooden plugs
- Paint
- Drapery approximately 1½ times the width of the mounting board

Instructions

1 Paint the board. Cut a dowel to fit the shank of each doorknob and extend ½ inch beyond the shank. Drill holes into but not through the board to receive each dowel, spacing the knobs about 12 inches apart. Secure the dowel to the board from the back using a countersunk screw.

2 Center the board over the window and bolt it to the wall, countersinking the bolts. Fill the holes with plugs and touch up the paint.

3 Make large buttonholes in the tops of the draperies, spacing them about 18 inches apart. The buttonholes should be about 3 inches long, large enough to slip easily over the doorknobs. Slip the draperies over the knobs as shown *below right*.

4 For the tiebacks, mount a doorknob on each side of the window frame, placing them about three-quarters of the way down the window frame.

You can't knock this look. Sparkling crystal **doorknobs** take the place of pegs on a simple Shaker-style rack. Oversized buttonholes make it easy to slip the panels in place.

So-so becomes so **fine** when sheer panels and a swag are stamped with a subtle floral design. Rubber stamps and ink pads made especially for fabric are available at stamping supply stores. Be sure to follow the ink manufacturer's instructions for fabric content, heat-setting, and laundering.

Stamp on It

Materials
- Sheer swag and side panels
- Rubber stamp and ink pad designed for use on fabric
- Kraft paper
- Low-tack painter's tape

Instructions

1 Prewash and dry the swag and panels to remove any sizing or finishes. Do not use fabric softener or detergent with fabric softener or stain-repellent additives. Lightly press the fabric using the appropriate heat setting for the type of fabric.

2 Smooth one section of a panel over kraft paper and tape it to your work surface. Using even pressure, randomly stamp the fabric. Do not rock the stamp. Re-ink the stamp each time. As you complete each section, replace the kraft paper and move to the next section.

3 For the striped border, mask off the lower 1 inch of the swag. Place the swag over kraft paper and press the stamp directly onto the fabric. Move along the edge, letting the color look mottled and uneven. When the ink dries, heat-set it according to the ink and drapery manufacturer's directions.

Have a Ball

Materials

- Two purchase sheer panels or one panel cut into two panels and hemmed
- Ball fringe trim
- Grommets larger than the rod
- Grommet tool
- Liquid ravel preventer

Instructions

1 Place the braid edge of the ball fringe over the inner hems of the panels and topstitch it in place. Turn under the raw edges of the braid at each end and treat the cut ends with liquid ravel preventer.

2 Mark the placement for the grommets on the curtain top, placing them about 8 inches apart. Install the grommets following the manufacturer's instructions and penetrating all layers of fabric.

3 Weave the curtain onto the rod. For a unified look, use a rod and tiebacks that repeat the ball design.

Add playful bounce to ordinary sheers with two throwbacks to the '60s, ball fringe and grommets. Both trims have made their way back into the decorating and fashion worlds and are considered trendy once again.

Score a winner with a contrasting topper for plain velvet panels. Each *pennant* is tipped with a tassel and tacked to the drapery. Satin buttons cover the stitching that holds the pennants to the panel. The topper here is also made of velvet, but any compatible combination of fabrics will work.

Making Points

Materials

- Velvet drapery fabric
- Lining to match the velvet
- Small upholstery tassels
- Satin-covered buttons

Instructions

1 Measure the width and length of the draperies. To make a pattern for the pennants, divide the width of each drapery panel into an even number and draw a horizontal line to that length. This is the upper edge of a pennant. For example, for a 48-inch-wide panel topped with six pennants, the line length would be 8 inches. For the depth of the pennant, divide the drapery panel length by 6. For example, for a 108-inch-long panel, the pennant would be 18 inches long. Intersect the first measurement (width) with the second (length) to form an upside down T. Connect the ends to form a triangle. Add ½-inch seam allowances to the pattern on all sides.

2 Cut the pennants from velvet and lining fabrics. With right sides facing, sew all around each triangle, leaving a small opening near the top for turning. Clip the corners, turn the triangles, and slipstitch the openings closed. Tack a tassel to the bottom point of each pennant.

3 Place the pennants over the panel and tack each in place at two points along the top edge. Sew a satin-covered button over each tacked spot.

Deep Borders

Materials

- Plain purchased unlined drapery panels
- Coordinating fabric for the lower bands
- Drapery fringe

Instructions

1 The drapery panels should measure four-fifths of the finished length. If necessary, trim the panels to 1½ inches below the edge of the window frame, or, if the windows extend to the floor, align the cutting line with a mullion (the horizontal molding supporting a window pane) and add ½ inch.

2 For the band, measure from the lower cut edge of the drapery to the floor. Add ½ inch for a seam allowance at the top and 4 inches for a hem. Measure the width of the panel and add 1 inch to each side for hems. Cut a band this size, piecing the fabric as needed.

3 Hem the sides of the band by turning under ½ inch, then ½ inch again and sewing it in place. For the bottom hem, turn up ½ inch, then 3½ inches and topstitch in place. Sew the bottom panel to the top panel, right sides facing, open out the curtain, and press the seam allowances down. Topstitch braid over the seamline.

If your windows and walls are too **tall** for standard draperies, extend them with a bottom band. A floral strip sewn to these plain panels brings the eye down to de-emphasize ceiling height and create coziness. In a room where windows stretch from floor to ceiling, hang the rods just below the crown molding to give the illusion of rich, fabric-covered *walls*.

Plain tab-topped panels take on a tailored appearance when trimmed with ribbon and accented with buttons. Use grosgrain ribbon and flat-finish buttons for a casual look or satin ribbon and shiny buttons for a more formal appearance.

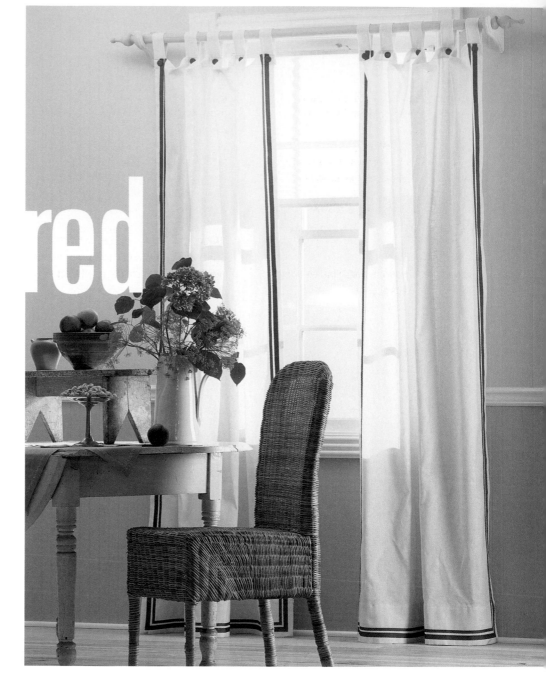

Ribbon-Trimmed Panels

Materials
- Plain tab-topped drapery panels
- ⅝-inch-wide and ⅜-inch-wide matching ribbons
- Fade-out fabric marker and ruler
- Fusible adhesive tape, fusible adhesive liquid, fabric glue, or sewing thread to match the ribbon
- Liquid ravel preventer (optional)
- Buttons to match the ribbon

Instructions

1 Cut the ribbons to fit the side and bottom edges of each panel, plus 1 inch at each end for turning to the back. Mark the placement for the ⅝-inch-wide ribbon ¾ inch from the side and bottom edges. Pin the ribbon to the panel, aligning the ribbon's outer edge with the placement line. Miter or butt the corners. If you butt the corners, treat each cut end with liquid ravel preventer. At the upper edge, turn under the raw edge ¼ inch and turn the remaining ribbon to the back of the panel. Fuse, glue, or sew the ribbon in place. *Note: If the drapes will be laundered or dry-cleaned often, stitch the ribbon for best results.*

2 Mark the line for the inner narrow ribbon ¼ inch from the edge of the first ribbon. Fuse, glue, or sew the narrow ribbon in place in the same manner as the wide ribbon.

3 Sew a button to the base of each tab.

Indoor Boxing

Materials

- Ready-made window box (available in garden departments or crafts stores)
- Paint
- Level and straightedge
- 2 or 3 decorative brackets to fit under the window box, depending on the length of the box
- Hardware for mounting the brackets
- Screws

Instructions

1 Paint the window box and brackets with two or more coats of paint.

2 Using a level and straightedge, mark where the bottom of the window box will fall. Mount the brackets to the wall, aligning the top of the brackets with this line. For best results, screw the brackets into studs or use anchor bolts. Make sure the brackets do not interfere with any structural supports on the bottom of the window box.

3 Place the window box on the brackets. Screw through the window box bottom and into the tops of the brackets in at least two places per bracket.

Who says window boxes have to be outdoors? Let purchased **window boxes** take the place of planters by mounting them under a sunny window inside the house. Place plastic pots with saucers or plastic box liners inside the window box to make maintaining and replacing the plants less messy.

Picket Line

Materials

- 1×4 pine boards
- 1×8 pine boards
- Wood glue
- Flat-head screws and 1¼-inch (3d) finish nails
- L-shape metal shelf brackets
- Paintable wood filler
- Paint
- Construction adhesive (optional)

Instructions

For the window box:

1 Make the window box slightly longer than the window's width. For simplicity, determine the size by planning the box length in 3½-inch increments (the width of a picket). If necessary, rip the back shorter than the front to accommodate the window trim.

2 Cut the front, bottom, and back from 1×8 boards as determined *above*. Cut two 6½-inch-long 1×8 pieces for the sides.

3 To assemble the box, glue and screw the front and back to the bottom, aligning the lower edges. Slide the end pieces into place and glue and screw them to the front, back, and bottom of the box.

4 Cut the 1×4 boards into 9½-inch lengths for the pickets. To make the points, mark down 2 inches on each side of one of the short ends. Mark the center of the short end. Joint the points to form a picket top. Cut along the lines. Cut enough pickets to go across the front plus three pickets for each side. Rip the last picket to fit.

5 Glue and nail the pickets to the box sides. Fit the first picket on each side flush with the front of the box and work toward the back. For the front, start at one end and work across the box, aligning the bottom of the pickets with the bottom of the box. Glue and nail the pickets in place. Countersink the nails, fill the holes, and touch up the paint.

6 Locate the studs below the window and mark the lower position of the window box. Screw the shelf brackets to the wall at this position to conceal the brackets and support the box. Set the window box on the brackets and screw it in place from the underside. Paint any exposed portion of the brackets.

For the picket wainscoting:

1 Measure the height of the pickets to align with the window box and rest on the baseboard. Cut the pickets to length and angle the tops as described in step 4 for the window box. Paint the pickets.

2 If the pickets are to be placed all around the room, start in the most visible corner of the room. For inside corners, cut a ³/₄×³/₄-inch spacer 2 inches shorter than the pickets. Attach it to the corner with construction adhesive. For outside corners, rip the picket to fit flush with the corner. Overlap the cut edge with the picket on the adjoining wall.

3 Starting at the designated corner, glue and nail the pickets so they rest on top of the baseboard. Countersink the nails, fill the holes, and retouch the paint.

For a room that is pointedly different, let pickets form the wainscot. Add a picket-covered window box for *garden*-fresh charm. Fill the window box with medium- to low-light plants such as ivy, croton, cyclamen, or kalanchoe.

Paint It Lacy

Materials

- Tape measure
- Lace, such as an old stained lace tablecloth or inexpensive yardage
- Stencil adhesive
- Painter's masking paper or kraft paper and low-tack painter's tape
- White enamel spray paint

Instructions

1 Measure the height and width of the glass. Cut a piece of lace to size, making the most of the pattern. Spray one side of the lace with stencil adhesive following the manufacturer's directions.

2 Clean the glass to make sure it is free from grease, film, or residue. Press the lace to the window and rub it with your hand to make sure it is tightly sealed. Mask off the window edges with painter's masking tape or kraft paper and tape.

3 Holding the can several inches from the glass and using long, slow strokes, spray a light coat of paint over the lace. Let the paint dry and apply a second light coat. When the paint is completely dry, remove the lace and masking paper. The painted surface can be gently washed. To remove the design, carefully scrape it off with a razor blade.

Note: Avoid painting the window on cold or humid days. The condensation will keep the paint from adhering.

An old **lace** tablecloth and some spray paint are the basic materials behind this delicate design. Place the lace over the window, spray-paint over the cloth, remove the lace and you have an intricate pattern that offers the privacy of frosted glass with a lot more style.

Window Ledge

Materials

- Purchased or handmade brackets
- 1×4 pine board
- Narrow decorative molding for shelf trim
- Screen molding for a plate rail (optional)
- Screws and finish nails
- Wood glue
- Paintable wood filler
- Paint

Instructions

1 Cut the 1×4 board and molding pieces to size. The shelf should extend beyond the window frame 1 to 2 inches on each side. Paint all the pieces, including the brackets.

2 Hold the shelf in place against the wall with the underside of the shelf resting on the top of the window frame. Draw a line on the underside of the shelf where the front edge of the window frame meets the shelf. At each end of the shelf, measure and mark 1 inch in from the side edge of the window frame. For a double window like the one shown, also mark the center. Remove the shelf and place the brackets along the marked lines. A small lip should extend beyond the back of the brackets. This will rest along the top of the window frame. Glue and screw the brackets in place, countersinking the screws. *Note:* Small windows need only two brackets. Large windows need three or more to prevent sagging.

3 Nail and glue the molding along the edges of the shelf, countersinking the nails. If you need a plate rail to keep items from slipping, nail screen molding to the top of the shelf at the depth desired for your collectibles.

4 Hold the shelf in place and drive screws from the top of the shelf directly into the top of the window frame. If more support is needed, insert screws at an angle through the brackets and into the window frame, alternating the direction of the screws. Fill all screw and nail holes and retouch the paint.

5 Place tension rods between the brackets to hold the window treatment.

Cap your window with a shelf fit to *display* your collectibles. Purchased brackets and a plain plank make the construction easy. Tension rods hold the valances in place. For more privacy, curtains, blinds, or decorative roller **shades** could step in for the valance.

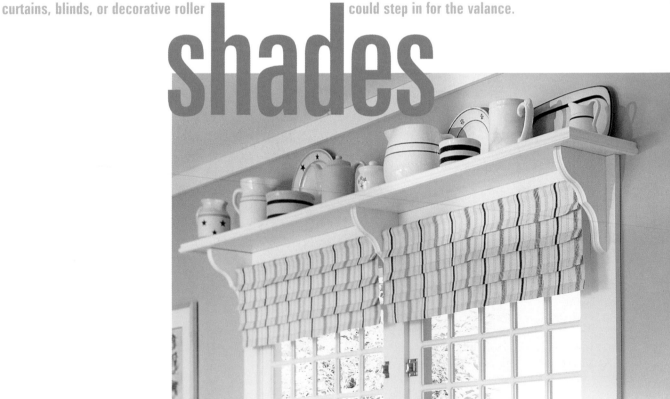

Valance Act

Materials

- Fabric deep enough to cover one-third to one-half the window and wide enough to swag gently and drape at the ends (the amount will vary with the window size)
- Ring tape and cord for Roman shades
- Purchased or self-made piping
- Coordinating fabric for the ruffle trim

Instructions

1 Narrowly hem the sides of the valance. Make a rod pocket in the top. Hang the valance in the window and mark the inside edge of the window frame. Sew the ring tape to the back of the valance along the marked lines. Tie the center of the cord to the lower ring on each side. Run one cord through the rings and leave the other cord free.

2 Baste the piping to the right side of the lower edge of the valance, aligning the lip of the piping with the raw edge of the valance fabric. The stitched edge of the piping should fall on the stitching line.

3 Cut a ruffle strip three times the measurement of the lower edge and double the desired depth, adding seam allowances to all sides. Fold the ruffle in half lengthwise, right sides facing. Sew across the short ends. Clip the corners, turn the ruffle to the right side, and press. Baste the raw edges together. Sew gathering stitches along the raw edges and pull up the gathers so the ruffle fits the valance bottom. With right sides facing and the piping sandwiched between the ruffle and the valance, sew the ruffle to the valance. *Note:* Sewing from the valance side and using a zipper foot will help keep the stitching close to the piping.

4 Clean-finish the raw edge and press the seam allowance toward the valance. Rehang the valance. Draw the cords to create the swag and tie the ends to the top ring.

Ring tape used on Roman shades defines the shape of this multipatterned valance. Two prints in the same color with an accent color for piping add interest to what is really just a simple swag.

Fringe Benefits

Materials

- Purchased valance *or* fabric deep enough to cover one-third to one-half the window and wide enough to swag gently and drape at the ends (the amount will vary with the window size)
- Ring tape and cording for Roman shades
- Acrylic beaded trim to fit the bottom edge of the valance

Instructions

1 If making your own valance, follow the instructions in step 1 of Valance Act valance on *page 113*. Narrowly hem the lower edge before attaching the ring tape.

2 Pin the hemmed edge of the valance over the tape of the trim and edgestitch the valance to the tape. Turn under the raw edges of the tape at each end.

3 Rehang the valance. Draw up the cords to create the desired amount of swag and tie the ends to the top ring.

Add sparkle and charm
with acrylic beaded fringe.

Sew your own valance or simply add trim to a purchased swag. Avoid sheer fabrics as the weight of the beads pulls lightweight fabric into a point instead of a gentle swoop.

A double layer of sheer fabric edged in piping drapes gracefully from decorative tiebacks. The bold hangers are as much a part of the *design* as the valance itself. Look for similar hardware at drapery and home decorating stores or substitute old doorknobs, cabinet knobs, or other hardware.

Pointedly Different

- Large sheet of paper for a pattern
- Water-erasable fabric marker
- Sheer polyester or polyester-blend fabric to measure 1½ times the width of the window and at least two-thirds the length of the window (the fabric amount will vary with the window size)
- Contrasting narrow piping
- Small tassels to match the piping
- 3 curtain tiebacks

Instructions

Note: The valance is made from one piece of fabric folded into a double layer. The fold forms the upper edge and the piping is sandwiched between the fabric layers at the lower stitched edge.

1 To make the pattern, draw the width of the valance 1½ times the width of the window. Mark the desired depth of the points, usually about one-third the height of the window. Leave the top and side edges straight and draw gently swooping points for the lower edge.

2 Fold the fabric in half crosswise, right sides facing. Trace the pattern onto the fabric, aligning the fold with the top edge of the pattern. Remove the pattern, but do not cut out the valance. Baste the piping to the side and lower edges of the right side of one layer of fabric following the marked lines.

3 Refold the fabric and sew the two layers together along the marked lines. Use a zipper foot to sew close to the piping and leave an opening for turning. Trim away excess fabric, turn the valance to the right side, and slipstitch the opening closed. Tack a tassel to the tip of each point.

4 Cut three 1½-inch ties from the fabric scraps. Fold the ties in half lengthwise, right sides facing, and sew along all raw edges, leaving an opening for turning. Turn, press, and slipstitch the opening closed. Fold the ties in half crosswise and tack them to the valance top at the outer edges and between each set of points.

5 Attach the tiebacks to the wall directly above the window frame. Tie the valance to the tiebacks.

Napkins and Rings

Materials

- Narrow curtain rod and mounting brackets
- Odd number of napkins in two coordinating patterns, one dark and one light or one plain and one patterned (the number will vary with the size of your window and the size of the napkins)
- Two more napkin rings than napkins

Instructions

1 Mount the brackets at the top of the window. Slide the napkin rings onto the rod and put the rod in place.

2 Fold the napkins in half diagonally. Starting with the dark or plain napkins, slide the napkin ends through the even-numbered napkin rings. Tuck the ends of the remaining napkins through the odd-numbered rings. Adjust the valance so some of the tails extend beyond the rings and the napkins swag slightly.

3 If necessary, tack the napkins to the rings on the back side to keep them from slipping out of place.

change

Take your linens to the top with a valance made from napkins and napkin rings. It takes only minutes to change the linens and rings, creating a quick valance for holidays, special occasions, or a of seasons.

the great outdoors

Extend your decorating to your outdoor **living** *areas.* **Creative** *containers, trellis walls, and loads of color perk up what is already one of your favorite* **places** *to unwind.*

Flower Buckets

Materials

- Galvanized buckets
- Low-tack painter's tape
- Sandpaper and tack cloth
- Metal primer
- Enamel paint
- Drill with a ⅜-inch bit (optional)
- Brass cup hooks (optional)

Instructions

1 If the buckets will be hung and do not have hanging holes, drill a ⅜-inch hole 1 inch from the top edge. Hang the buckets from cup hooks after they are painted.

2 Clean and dry the buckets thoroughly. Mask off the upper third of each bucket. Lightly sand below the tape and wipe each bucket clean. Paint the sanded area with metal primer and two or more coats of enamel paint. Apply the paint with long, smooth strokes so it's perfectly even.

3 For vase-style buckets, check to see if the container is watertight. If not, line the bucket with a plastic container, tumbler, or a heavy-duty plastic storage bag before adding flowers and water. For planter buckets, drill a ⅜-inch drainage hole in the bottom. Cover the hole with a piece of screen or shard of broken pot before adding potting soil.

Galvanized **buckets** from the hardware store or garden center take a dip in popsicle-bright paint. Hang them from a fence, line them up along a walk or rail, or employ one or two for a **centerpiece**. Use them for cut flowers or add a drainage hole and use them for growing plants.

Tubby-Time Fun

Instructions

1 Clean and dry the tub thoroughly. Mask off the upper portion of the tub, following the tub's embossed lines. Lightly sand below the tape and wipe the bucket clean. Paint the sanded area with metal primer, then apply two or more coats of white enamel paint.

2 Divide the circumference of the tub into an even number of stripes. Mask off the stripes and paint them two or more coats of the contrasting color. Remove the tape.

3 If the tub will be used for planting, add drainage holes. Drill one or more ¼-inch diameter holes in the bottom. Cover them with screen or shards of broken pots before adding potting soil and plants.

Awning-style stripes brighten a galvanized tub and provide a playful way to display plants. Paint tubs of several sizes and use them for ice, beverages, and toys.

Perked-Up Percolator

Materials

- Old metal coffeepot
- Metal primer (optional)
- White enamel paint (optional)
- Acrylic paint in yellow, blue, and white or the desired colors
- Paintbrushes: 1-inch foam, flat, and liner
- Water-based spray sealer

Instructions

Note: The coffeepot *below* was originally white enamel with rust showing through. If your coffeepot is not white, apply metal primer and white enamel paint. To expose some rust, lightly sand the paint from some areas. For a newer look, prime the coffeepot and paint it with two or more coats of white enamel paint. Do not sand the paint.

1 Clean the coffeepot thoroughly. Mix blue and white paints in a ratio of two parts blue to one part white. Thin the paint with water until it is the consistency of ink. Using the foam brush, paint vertical stripes around the pot, spacing them fairly evenly.

2 Using undiluted blue paint and a liner brush, add a thin line of blue to the left of each wide stripe. Let the paint dry.

3 Mix equal amounts of yellow and white paint. Thin the paint until it is the consistency of ink. Using the flat brush, paint several horizontal stripes around the pot, spacing the lines fairly evenly.

4 After the paint dries, apply two coats of spray sealer to protect the paint.

An old *enamel* coffeepot that spent its early years on the campfire serves a new purpose as a folksy plaid vase. A simple painted design provides the facelift. To keep the horizontal lines even, wrap a piece of stiff paper around the pot and use its lower edge as a painting guide. Start at the top and move the paper down to paint succeeding lines, letting each line dry before painting the next one.

Vines seem to climb like magic when the structure fades into the background. A wire *grid* is the trick here, letting the bright blossoms wind their way within the wooden framework. Because the wires are nearly invisible, the flowers can take center stage.

High-Wire Climbers

Materials

- Two 23-inch-long pressure-treated 2×4s
- Three 8-foot-long pressure-treated 1×4s
- Portable circular saw with a rip guide or a table saw
- 1¼-inch and 2-inch deck screws
- ½-inch roofing nails
- 30 feet of 14-gauge solid, bare copper electrical wire
- Weatherproof glue
- Exterior-grade paint and primer
- Crushed rock

Instructions

Follow the construction diagrams. Paint all pieces before assembly. Drill pilot holes to prevent splitting the lumber.

1 Using a circular saw or table saw, cut decorative grooves into the face of each 1×4 post as shown in the photo *opposite*.

2 Cut a 2×4 to length for the upper and lower caps, then notch them with repeated side-by-side saw cuts. Cut the upper and lower rails to length from 1×4s. Rip the upper rail 2½ inches wide.

3 Assemble the posts, rails, and caps with glue and screws, spacing them as shown on the diagram. Drive all screws from the back, using 2-inch screws to hold the posts to the lower cap and 1¼-inch screws for all the other assembly.

4 Cut the 1×2 upper cap, upper and lower filler, and the trim to size. Glue and screw them into position. Place the trellis facedown on a work surface. Partially drive roofing nails around the perimeter every 4 inches, making sure nails align with each other across the posts. (If they're not aligned, the grid of wires won't be square.)

5 To string the horizontal wires, loop copper wire twice around the top nail in one of the posts. Wrap the end of the wire around itself to secure it. Run the wire to the nail directly opposite and wind the wire around the nail twice. Run the wire to the nail below, wrap it twice, and run the wire to the opposite nail. Continue stringing the wire in this manner to create the horizontal lines of the grid. Pull the wire just tight enough to keep it straight but avoid excess tension. End the wire in the same way as you began. String the vertical wire to the back of the trellis in the same manner.

6 Dig 24-inch-deep holes for the trellis. Put 4 inches of crushed rock in the bottom for drainage. Hold the trellis plumb and backfill the holes. Tamp the soil with a 2×4.

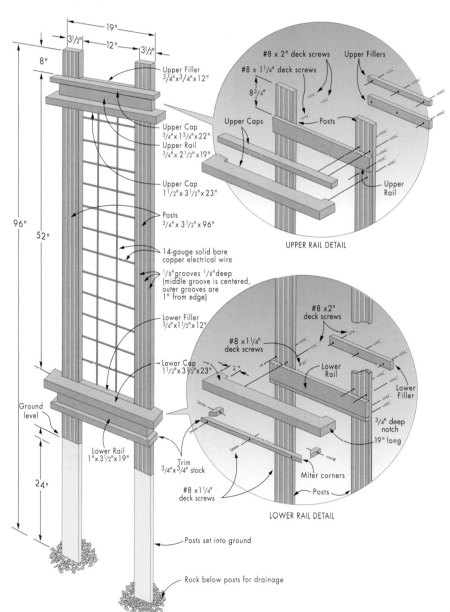

Create **privacy** or block an unsightly view with a row of vine-covered trellises. Place them at angles like half-open shutters or line them up shoulder-to-shoulder for total solitude.

Trellis Trio

Materials

- Eight 8-foot-long pressure-treated 2×4s
- Sixteen 8-foot-long pressure-treated 1×2s
- 6-foot-long pressure-treated 2×10
- Two 1×2 brackets
- 1¼-inch and 2-inch deck screws
- Weatherproof glue
- Exterior-grade primer and paint
- Saw with miter capabilities
- Drill with countersink bit
- Crushed rock

Instructions

Follow the diagrams for construction details. Paint all pieces before assembly. Drill pilot holes to prevent splitting the lumber.

1 Cut a 30-degree angle at the top end of each 2×4 post. Cut the two 1×2 brackets; glue and nail each to the inner face of a post, centering it side-to-side and with the top end 1½ inches from the angled cut.

2 Create pointed tips for each of the 1×2 trellis uprights with 45-degree cuts, then cut the uprights to length. Crosscut the 1×2 trellis rails, then nail together the trellis rails and uprights into a lattice assembly.

3 Cut the 2×4 top rail to length; position it between the posts and drive deck screws into countersunk pilot holes from the back. Nail the lattice assembly to the brackets.

4 Complete the assembly by cutting the roof pieces and screwing them into position. For the arched trellis, cut the post tops square as shown in the alternate roof detail. Glue together two 2×10s. Use a string and pencil to draw the radius. For the peaked top, join the two sides in a 30-degree angle.

5 Dig two 28-inch holes for each trellis. Place 4 inches of crushed rock in each hole for drainage. Hold the trellis plumb while backfilling the hole with dirt. Firmly tamp the soil with a 2×4.

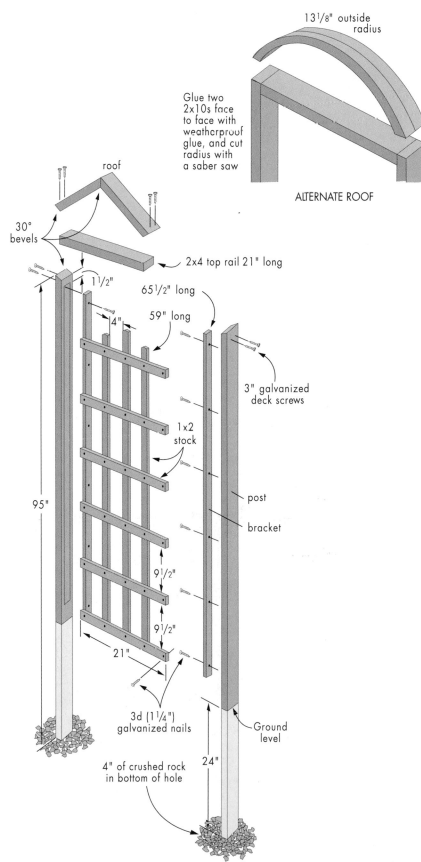

13⅛" outside radius

Glue two 2x10s face to face with weatherproof glue, and cut radius with a saber saw

ALTERNATE ROOF

roof

30° bevels

2x4 top rail 21" long

1½"

65½" long

4"

59" long

3" galvanized deck screws

1x2 stock

95"

post

bracket

9½"

9½"

21"

3d (1¼") galvanized nails

4" of crushed rock in bottom of hole

Ground level

24"

Flower Box Seat

Materials

- Old chair with a small rim or strapping bands across the seat to support the box
- 1×4 pine board
- Exterior-grade plywood scrap
- Wood glue
- Nails
- Clamps
- Drill
- Exterior grade sealer
- Window screen scrap

Instructions

1 Cut the 1×4 board to make a box that fits inside the chair seat. Glue and nail the corners using butt joints. Clamp the joints until the glue dries.

2 Cut a base from exterior-grade plywood. Glue and nail it to the box frame. Drill drainage holes through the bottom.

3 Seal the box with exterior-grade sealer. Line the bottom with window screen before adding potting soil and plants.

Guests will sit up and take notice when they see a flower-covered chair **seat** made up of real plants. Look for old chairs with missing or damaged cushions and seats, then build a simple box to hold the flowers.

Clean-finish: To treat the raw edge of a fabric so it does not fray and has a neater appearance. The most common methods are to turn under and stitch the raw edge or to zigzag or serge the raw edge.

Clip art: Artwork (mostly line drawings) that is copyright-free and available for purchase. Most images are available in books, categorized by theme, and found at art supply stores. There are also online sources. Because the images are copyright-free, you can legally photocopy them for use on any kind of art, crafts, and decorating projects.

Dauber: A small shaped sponge that is on a handle. The sponge is generally shaped like a half-sphere and forms a round dot pattern when dipped in paint and stamped onto a surface. Daubers come in different sizes.

Edgestitch: To sew very closely (about ¹⁄₁₆ inch) to a fold or hem edge.

Glaze: A transparent liquid that is mixed with paint to make the paint more translucent, add depth, and lengthen the open (wet) time so faux finishes can be applied before the paint dries. Glaze comes in both latex and oil-based forms. Be sure to match your glaze type to your paint type.

Grommet tool: The tool needed for applying grommets to fabric. There are two basic types: pliers and hammer. The pliers squeeze the two pieces of the grommet together, and the hammer places the pieces in special cups to protect them as you pound them together.

Heat-set: To make something permanent with the use of heat. The most common heat-set item is textile paint. Many paint manufacturers recommend ironing a painted item for a certain period of time to make the paint bond to the fabric and prevent bleeding and fading when the fabric is laundered. Some glass and tile paints also require heat-setting to make them permanent.

Hook-and loop-tape: A two-piece tape for temporarily joining two objects together. One side is made up of a soft, fuzzy material and the other consists of rigid plastic loops that grasp and hook into the soft side. The tapes can be pressed together and pulled apart repeatedly. Hook-and-loop tape comes in self-adhesive and sew-in varieties or a combination of the two. Trade name: Velcro®.

Liquid ravel preventer: A clear gluelike liquid that seals the raw edges of fabric and prevents or reduces fraying. When applied correctly, it is washable, flexible, and invisible. It may need to be reapplied after repeated washings. If applied too heavily, it becomes stiff and may be slightly visible.

Miter: To fit together at a specific angle. The most common angle is 45 degrees. Miters can be folded (as in the case of fabrics) or cut (as in the case of wood).

Pressure-treated: Chemically treated wood that has been made more rot- and decay-resistant through the use of pressure. The chemicals used are often toxic and so is the sawdust. Wear a protective mask when cutting, sanding, or handling pressure-treated wood and sawdust. Never burn pressure-treated wood, as it may give off toxic smoke.

Rod pocket: The casing or pocket at the top of a curtain or valance panel designed for holding the curtain rod.

Slipstitch: To invisibly handsew two pieces of fabric together, usually along an edge left open for turning. The needle is woven back and forth between the folded edges, taking small stitches and sliding the needle underneath the folded edge.

Stock molding: Any shaped wooden trim that home improvement centers and lumber yards commonly carry. Typical examples of stock molding are crown molding, screen molding, chair rail, quarter-round, half-round, and windowsill.

Textile medium: A liquid that is mixed with acrylic paint to help the paint bond to fabric. Mixing textile medium with acrylic paint will keep the paint softer and more flexible when it dries. Textile medium also helps prevent bleeding and fading when laundering the item.

Topstitch: To machine-stitch along the right side of an item so the stitching is visible. The stitching may be functional, decorative, or both. Topstitching is often used for machine-stitched hems or to give a finished look to a folded edge.

Welt: Fabric-covered cording that has a flat lip that extends beyond the round cord. The lip is used to sew the cording into the seamline. Welt is also called piping, cording with a lip, or cording with a flange.

the right glue for you

Choosing the proper adhesive can be a sticky situation. The trick is to match the glue to the job. No one adhesive is perfect for all projects. Check the adhesives aisles of home improvement and crafts stores frequently. New products are added constantly, each designed with a specific purpose in mind.

Epoxy: This two-part adhesive consists of a catalyst and a hardener. The glue will not work until the two elements are combined. Some come as two separate components that you mix, some are in a double-syringe with a plunger, and others are in separate tunnels within a tube and combine as soon as you squeeze them out. Epoxy is a good all-purpose adhesive for many projects, including gluing wood, ceramic, and glass. Many epoxy glues have flammable fumes and should not be placed near a heat source or open flame until completely dry.

Fabric glue: Liquid fabric glue is generally clear, flexible, and washable. Some will not withstand dry cleaning so always check the label. Fabric glue is meant to glue two fabrics together. Other glues are available for gluing items such as gems or jewels to fabric.

Hot glue: Low-temp, high-temp, and dual-temp glue guns each require their own kind of glue stick. Glue guns are easy to use and the glue sets quickly, but the bond is not always long-lasting. Cold may cause the glue to crack, high heat may soften it, and it does not withstand laundering or dry cleaning. If the glue sets too quickly, it may leave a ridge. Specialty glue sticks such as glitter glue and wood glue are also available.

Mastic: This general term applies to thick construction adhesives. Mastic comes in cans or caulking-gun style and is spread with a notched trowel. It is used for bonding large items such as paneling, tile, flooring, or drywall to wood, metal, or masonry.

Thick white crafts glue: This all-purpose glue is thicker than regular white glue. It does not soak into porous surfaces as easily as ordinary white glue and is easy to brush on for smooth application. It works on most porous surfaces.

Weatherproof glue: Designed for gluing outdoor wood projects, weatherproof glue resists moisture, chemicals, and temperature changes.

Wood glue: This strong glue is used for most woodworking projects. It has medium heat and moisture resistance and has excellent gap-filling characteristics, making it a good choice for joining two rough surfaces that have small open spaces between them.

index